10/2000

God is faithful. Always!

Warren

The Foolishness
of God

Nola Warren

D1238613

CREATION
HOUSE
PRESS

THE FOOLISHNESS OF GOD by Nola Warren
Published by Creation House Press
A part of Strang Communications Company
600 Rinehart Road
Lake Mary, Florida 32746
www.creationhouse.com

Unless otherwise noted, all Scripture quotations are from the King
James Version of the Bible.

Library of Congress Card Number: 00-107155
ISBN: 0-88419-751-4 (paperback)

0 1 2 3 4 5 6 7 VERSA 8 7 6 5 4 3 2 1
Printed in the United States of America

DEDICATION

To Frank, my knight in shining, white armor.

ACKNOWLEDGMENTS

My sincere thanks and appreciation to all those who stood with me during the nearly four years of widowhood: my mom and dad, Eugene and Lorene Holder; my sister and her husband, David and Rena Pitman; my brother, W.W. Holder; the two young ladies who laid aside their personal plans for a period of time and made my life their own, Ruth McEwen and Ruthie Fried; and the entire faculty, staff and student body of International Bible College. A special word of thanks also to the missionary community in Durango who were such a source of strength during those years: Richard and Juliet Milk (Methodist missionaries), Gilbert and Carolyn Ross (Baptist missionaries), and Dan and Eleanor Petker, Richard and Delores Wiens, Eugene and Lillian Janzen, and Willie and Betty Heinrich, all missionaries with the Reformed Mennonite Church of North America. All these people helped make those years possible.

There are no words to express my appreciation and thanks to my friend, Lorraine Peterson, who first challenged me about writing this book and then coached me through the entire process. Thank you, Lorraine. I value your friendship.

TABLE OF CONTENTS

Introduction 6

1. In the Beginning 9

2. "Here We Are, You Lucky People" 30

3. The End of the Beginning 49

4. In the Meantime…. 63

5. Picking Up the Pieces.....................................74

6. "¡Asi es la Vida!" 87

7. Victory and Defeat.......................................104

8. All in God's Time 119

Epilogue 138

INTRODUCTION

It was a winter day, New Year's Eve, in northern Mississippi. The wind was blowing, and the temperature had been below freezing since the night before, when the young wife went into labor. The mother-to-be was seventeen years old. This was her first baby, and the whole thing turned out to be more of a problem than she had expected. Estranged from her parents because of their objection to her bridegroom, she had eloped almost two years earlier, and there had been no contact between the two families from that time until she went into labor. That was when the young husband sent word to his in-laws, and they came to watch with their daughter all during the long night. The country doctor was also sent for and got up from his seat beside the fireplace from time to time to check on the wife. The pains had been coming for well over thirteen hours, and still the baby was not born. A couple of hours earlier, they had gotten stronger, and the doctor and the wife's mother had taken her into the kitchen, where there was a table they could put her on in preparation for the delivery. The doctor said the old bed in the front room was too saggy. He had to have a higher, firmer surface from which to work.

It had been a while since those waiting in the front room heard anything from the kitchen. They weren't talking to one another, either. The girl's father was aching inside that his beautiful, obedient daughter had been brought to such low circumstances. She had always been close to him, and his heart broke when he thought about her childhood and life at home before this young 'upstart' came along and stole her affection. All her life, she had been the most obedient of all their children, but when she turned sixteen, she got it into her head that she had to marry this man. And she did. In spite of her father's effort to stop them, they eloped. He had chased behind them for hours trying to stop them before it was too late. He chased them down country roads, across boggy fields and into the next county. He chased them all day and finally returned home defeated. They were married late that afternoon.

It had been a hard two years—hard for the family who lost its lovely daughter to a man they considered unworthy, and hard on the young couple who had to make a start during the last of the depression years in northern Mississippi. There had been times when they only ate cornbread and molasses for weeks at a time. But they had made it, and now their first child was being born.

Although the young wife was in the adjoining room, she could hear her daddy pacing the floor and praying all during her labor. It brought back to her all the times he had spent the night walking the floor and praying for her when she was sick. It especially reminded her of the time she had double pneumonia and nearly died because penicillin was not available. She had been unconscious for several hours during that ordeal but had moments of lucidity, when, for a few seconds, she knew what was going on. Over the period of some 48 hours of unconsciousness and deliriousness, whenever she had a few seconds of clarity, she remembered her father's being there beside her bed and holding onto her life through prayer. He was doing it again as she tried to give birth.

Suddenly there was the sound of quick action from the kitchen. Voices were raised, people were moving around, chairs were scooted back and the soon-to-be grandmother was giving unsolicited instructions to the doctor to make sure he did this job right. Then came the sound they had all been waiting for: the cry of a newborn baby. It was a girl. The baby didn't cry long; she was too busy looking around at everyone and trying to decide what kind of world she had been born into.

The weather was still freezing, and the wind was still blowing so hard that sometimes it lifted the linoleum rug off the floor—but that was all forgotten. The ordeal and waiting of the past 13 hours was forgotten. The animosity of the grandparents toward this young man who had taken their beautiful daughter from them was forgotten. The hurt of the young mother because of her parents' rejection was forgotten. The hurt of the baby's father because his wife's parents didn't think he was good enough for their daughter was forgotten. All those things were forgotten as they gathered around the mother and her baby girl. There were tears, smiles and lots of joy as they rejoiced in this baby, whose birth had healed the breach between the two families. It was a breach that never opened again.

Since they had been married for almost two years before the first baby was born, everyone thought the young couple might not have any more children, so everyone wanted to get in on the naming of the child. Her paternal grandmother suggested "Wanda," her maternal grandmother gave her own name, "Nola," and her father gave her an abbreviation of his name, "Jean." They named her Wanda Nola Jean. She was the first of nine children.

****

Months later in Amarillo, Texas, another young couple discovered that their first baby was on the way. It was the same day Pearl Harbor was bombed. This mother-to-be was also a teenager, but apart from that, there weren't any similarities between the two couples. The United States was well into World War II, and his father was already enlisted in the U.S. Army when this baby was born in a hospital in north central Texas on August 5, 1942. When the young parents were told they had a son, they told the doctor that they wanted to name him Jerry but that they hadn't been able to come up with a second name.

"Why not name him Douglas, for General Douglas MacArthur?" the doctor asked. And that's how Jerry Douglas Witt got his name.

Only God knew how the future of these two families would be eternally tied together through the lives of these two babies.

1

In the Beginning

"Nola Jean"

Growing up as the oldest in a family of nine children is no easy task. We were a close family, with grandparents, uncles and aunts all involved in our lives and we learned early in life about God and the importance of the church. There was never much money around, but we usually had what we needed, and we all knew how to work hard. The four oldest children were girls, and our parents saw to it that we avoided worldly amusements, dressed like Christians and only dated believers.

People often ask, "Were there fights between you children?"

Not the kind that became physical. Our dad had drilled into us the idea that anyone involved in a physical fight would give account to him, and giving account to Daddy was something we avoided at all costs. So, "No, there weren't many physical fights between us."

However, we were all born with the gift of talking and we learned early in life how to defend ourselves with our tongues. Some interesting arguments developed. One of the biggest conflicts that developed between the four older children—all girls—was about clothes. I never was a person who borrowed or wanted to lend my clothing to anyone, not even to one of my younger sisters. But, sometimes they would "borrow" things without permission, and I wouldn't know about it until I found a dirty dress in my closet. On one occasion, I discovered a blouse that my sister had worn, dirtied, torn and then hung back in the closet. I knew who the guilty party was, so I called her into my bedroom, showed her the blouse and began to admonish her about doing things like that. As I continued talking to her, she got in my face with her index finger rubbing against her thumb, all the time whining out a little tune. Finally I asked her, "What in the world is that supposed to be?"

Grinning like a little imp, she said, "That's the smallest violin in the world playing 'My Heart Bleeds Peanut Butter for You!' "

We both began to laugh, and that broke up my lecture on not borrowing my clothes without permission.

Some people might think my parents were too strict, but I don't remember feeling penned in or deprived. We had lots of fun, and I enjoyed life a good deal. No doubt if we had really set out to deceive Mom and Dad, we could have, but we had the fear of Daddy well programmed into our minds, and we weren't interested in going down that road. Daddy was the authority figure, and Mama was our "intercessor." But even more than Mom and Dad, there was God, and we were taught to love and serve Him from the day we were born.

Until my sophomore year in high school, I wasn't too concerned about any future education; I was too busy having fun. But, sometime during my junior year of high school, I began to realize that I enjoyed studying, discovering new things and talking with my teachers, and that graduating from high school was not going to be enough. I wanted to go to college.

Actually, that was no problem. My parents were in favor of it. I was an honor graduate from high school with several scholarship opportunities, and I was excited about going to college. Then, when I moved into my senior year of high school and we began to get down to the "nitty gritty" of where I would go to college, my dad came up with one of his rules. At first, he said I would have to go to school somewhere close enough for me to come home every weekend. That was bad enough. But then he changed that and said I couldn't go away to college in another town and live with people he didn't know. I would have to stay at home and attend college at one of the local schools. I wasn't happy about it, but I knew that unless something happened to change Daddy's mind, that's the way it would be.

At seventeen, I had a lot of excitement and interest shut up in my bones, a real desire to know more and do more, to meet new people and to see new places. But unless something happened to change my daddy's mind, I knew I would have to stay at home and go to school during the day. I don't remember actually praying about it, but God must have seen the real desire I had for more, and He answered. We discovered International Bible College in San Antonio, Texas. My dad flew down to San Antonio, visited the school, met the college president and came back saying that I could go. It wasn't until I actually arrived in San Antonio and was arranging my class schedule that I realized this was not a liberal arts college, but rather a Bible college.

Some people might say, "How sad. Here is an honor graduate with scholarship opportunities, and she winds up more than 1,000 miles from home in a small, non-accredited Bible college studying theology."

But God had everything under control. He knew where He wanted me and what He wanted me to do. So He used the fact that IBC was the only place my dad would let me go to school away from home and set my feet on the road He had planned for me all along.

So, at seventeen years old, I wound up a freshman at IBC and working to pay my way through school. I loved it. All the time I was in high school, I had been accepted by my teachers and fellow students, but I was still not part of the group because of my Christian standards. The church my dad had founded and was pastoring was still small at that time and didn't have many young people in it. No one from my school went to church with me. So, although I didn't have any hang-ups or feelings of rejection, I was still not part of the group at school. I was not included in their plans for parties, movies, dances, joy rides, etc...

Then, at IBC, I found this group of students who was just as fanatic about the things of God as I was. I felt like I had arrived in heaven. They were all Christians, they had basically the same standards I had, and they were my friends. I danced through every day. I sang all the time. There was a joy that bubbled inside me and everything I did. One day at work while I was filing some account cards, I hadn't even realized I was singing until my boss asked me if I would mind turning the radio off. I loved everybody. The world was a beautiful place. God was a great God, life was a challenge, and everything was perfect! To all my teachers who thought I was "giddy," I can now tell them I was happy and loved every minute of my time at IBC. I joined the choir, the orchestra, the drama club, home missions and foreign missions prayer groups—everything! I just wanted everything I could get, so I went for everything.

When I first arrived at IBC, I learned that they needed someone to work in the office on campus, and since I had worked in my dad's office since I was ten years old, could take shorthand as well as type eighty words per minute and knew bookkeeping, I felt certain the job was mine. Imagine my surprise when they turned me down. One of my friends who did get the job told me later that they had said: "She's too silly, too giddy. She laughs and cuts up too much. She'd have this office in a state of turmoil all the time."

So, I didn't get the job there on campus, but I got an even better one, which I held for more than five years.

Although I was not opposed to the idea, there were no boyfriends. I was writing a fellow in the Marines, and the relationship could be classified as semi-serious, but at IBC, I didn't have a boyfriend. Many friends, but no boyfriends.

One of these friends was a fellow named Archie. Archie was from Pennsylvania and was a hemophiliac[1]. Everybody loved Archie, a big tease. He didn't have a girlfriend, so we kept each other company. One night as we were all coming back from some activity on the school bus, Archie was sitting beside me, and all the students in our area were laughing and having a good time. Suddenly, somebody brought up a controversial subject, and we all got into this big discussion. Naturally, I wound up right in the middle of it. Archie sat grinning and watching me "expound," and suddenly he burst into laughter. He was laughing at me.

Turning to look at him, I asked, "What is so funny?"

"You are," he said.

"I am? Why am I so funny?"

"Because," he said, "you're always saying you don't have any particular call on your life, but I know what you're going to be."

By this time, he was laughing again with his head thrown back, and I was sitting there with my mouth hanging open.

"You," Archie proclaimed, "are going to be a lady preacher."

"Never, never, never," I screeched. "Never will I be a lady preacher."

In my mind, a lady preacher was a woman who was at least 200 pounds overweight, wore long-sleeved white dresses, had her hair pulled back in a tight bun, sweated when she preached, had a small mustache and henpecked her husband.

Refusing the "call" that Archie had put on me, I banged him on the head with my Bible and repeated, "Never!"

Archie sat there looking at me with a gleam in his eye and a grin still on his face, and said, "You just wait and see."

****

The wind was cold that memorable December morning as I ran across campus from the girls' dormitory to the dining hall. It was still dark, but I had to get up early to do my "sharework."[2] My job was to set the tables for breakfast and then wait tables.

My heart was happy and light, and I went about my job with a song and a bounce. I had been at IBC for a little more than three months, and, as far as I was concerned, it was still a little piece of heaven on earth. I was just glad that I was alive and in San Antonio at IBC.

Some of the students had the habit of arriving at the dining hall a little before serving time. They waited in the vestibule until all was ready and the bell rang for breakfast. That particular morning, there was only one such brave person out in the cold so early—a new fellow sitting in the telephone booth. In the midst of the breakfast preparations, I noticed him and went over to introduce myself.

"Hi!" I said. "My name is Nola Jean Holder. Are you a new student?"

"I'm Jerry Witt," was the reply, "and, no, I am not a new student—at least not yet. I'm here with my dad visiting and I'm thinking about enrolling at mid-term."

"Well, I certainly hope you do," I said. "We have some great times here. I know you'll enjoy it just like the rest of us do."

As I excused myself and continued on with my work, I thought to myself, *Hmmmm. Not bad! Tall, dark curly hair, blue eyes and a beautiful smile. I hope he does come back to school.*

There was no forewarning or any idea that the young man with whom I had just spoken so casually would change my entire life.

"JERRY"

Jerry was the oldest of three children raised in Texas, California and Mexico. His mother and father had given their hearts to the Lord not long after Jerry was born. They had pastored a church in St. Jo, Texas, during his childhood. It was while they were there that Dave and Reba Witt began to feel that God had something more He was asking of them, and they began to make plans to move to Mexico to become involved in missionary work. Dave had met some people who were "flying" missionaries, and that appealed to him, so he set about getting his first airplane and moving his family to the Republic of Mexico.

The plane was used to fly into remote areas of the country with no Gospel witness and drop Gospels of St. John to the villagers. It was for this purpose that Dave and Reba gathered their family, (by this time, there were three children) and moved to Durango, Mexico. Jerry was nine years old.

Jerry had always desired the things of God, but as he began to go into his teen years, he entered a time of rebellion. He got into mischief running around with other teenagers in the city. Dave and Reba were worried, and they held onto God for their oldest son and refused to give him up.

When Jerry was fourteen, the friction between he and his parents had been building up to a pretty steady boil, and he and his dad had a big confrontation. As a result, Jerry re-dedicated his life to the Lord and left on a trip with his father to central Texas for missionary services. After that, they were on their way back to Mexico when they "just happened" to pass through San Antonio on a Sunday evening.

It was late one Sunday afternoon when they arrived in San Antonio, and not knowing anything about the city, they found themselves in the downtown area on East Houston Street. Dave felt he needed a tie to wear to a church service, so they parked the car and went into some stores to look for a tie. Jerry and Dave separated and agreed to meet back at the car within thirty minutes. Jerry walked into Walgreens drug store on the corner of East Houston and Navarro streets. After wandering the aisles of the store for a while, he realized he wasn't going to find what they were looking for there and decided to give it up and go back to meet his dad. As he walked out of Walgreens, he saw that a group of young people had gathered on the street corner. They had an accordion, guitars and Bibles. They would sing a song, and then one of the young men would step out and give a short testimony of what Jesus had done in his life. As he stood watching, to Jerry's amazement, none other than his father stepped out and began to tell what God had done in his life. His dad had discovered the group sooner than Jerry and was already involved in the street service. A few minutes later, the students (from IBC) finished their activities and invited Jerry and Dave to go along with them to Revival Temple for the Sunday night service. From there, they went to the IBC campus and spent the night. The next morning, they were in the dining hall for breakfast.

****

After speaking to Jerry on that cold December morning in the dining hall, I excused myself and continued my work. By this time, more students were coming into the dining hall, and as Jerry looked around for a familiar face, he found the only person he knew on the entire campus, another missionary kid from Monterrey, Mexico. Jerry grabbed Mickey by the arm and pulled him over to the door leading into the dining area and asked, "Who is that girl setting the tables for breakfast?"

Mickey stuck his head a little farther around the door to see better and then said: "Oh. That's Nola Jean. But you needn't get interested in her because she has a 'steady' in the Marines. Besides that, she's three years older than you."

"It doesn't matter," Jerry answered, smiling. "I'll marry her some day."

During those years, IBC was not only a Bible College, but it also had a high school department. It was in the high school that Jerry enrolled a few weeks later and became an integrated part of the fabric that makes up the history of IBC. He became well-known because of his individuality, good looks and temper. Because of the difference in our grade levels, the only class we had together was choir, and he was soon singled out as a good tenor.

"COURTSHIP"

It wasn't long before word began to seep through to me that Jerry said he was going to marry me. He wasn't obnoxious about it, but he never did change his mind. He had other girlfriends, but everyone knew that it was Nola Jean that he planned to marry. Of course, all the students laughed at him whenever he said things like that because he was still a lowly high school student, and I was in college.

I didn't laugh. In fact, I enjoyed it. I honestly felt that what he was experiencing was a normal teenager's crush and that he would soon recover. So, although I enjoyed being with him, I didn't respond to his romantic ideas—partly because of our ages and partly because I did have a 'steady' in the Marines.

Not long after Jerry came to IBC, my 'steady' left on a tour of duty in Japan. He was to be gone for 18 months. Just before he left, he called me from California and sent me a big box of candy and a colored portrait of himself. I received both of those packages just as I arrived home from work one afternoon, and I took them over to the dining hall with me. Although the evening meal was almost finished, several of the students were still around, and Jerry was one of them. I passed the candy around to everyone and showed the picture of my handsome Marine to everyone who would look. When the picture was passed to Jerry, he looked at it for a few minutes, and then with a twinkle in his eyes, he looked up at me and winked.

"Good-looking guy," he said. "If it weren't for the fact that I know the Lord's on my side, I might just give up."

That fall found Jerry back at IBC, but I was still in Georgia. My parents didn't want me to go back to school that fall, so I decided to accept a job offer. I was to be at work the next morning, but during the night, God spoke to me.

Up until now, I hadn't felt any particular destiny or call concerning my presence at IBC, nor did I feel any special call to the ministry. I had gone because it was where I could go. Now, suddenly, the night before I was to report to my new job, God was speaking to me, and He wanted me to go back to IBC. Wrestling with the problem I didn't sleep that night. At daybreak, I got up and went downstairs to my parents' bedroom. Mom was already getting everybody off to work and school, but Dad was still in the bedroom. As I sat down in the chair in their bedroom, I burst into tears and asked "Daddy, can I talk to you?"

Surprise and compassion written all over his face, he said, "Of course you can talk to me. What's wrong?"

I said, "Daddy, I can't take that job. I've got to go back to IBC." By this time, the tears were really flowing.

My dad said, "You don't have to take that job if you don't want to. And if you really feel like you need to go back to IBC, then that's what you can do."

It was like an enormous burden had been lifted from my spirit.

Then I asked another question. "Daddy, will you explain to Mama about why I can't take the job?"

"Yes," he said. "I'll talk to your Mother about it."

Then I asked another favor.

"Daddy, would you please also call Sarah (the lady who had gotten me the work and with whom I was to work) and let her know that I won't be taking the job?"

"Yes," he said. "I'll do that also."

My dad stood with me in that decision, and although he wasn't happy about my going off one thousand miles to school again, he understood that God was dealing with me, and he respected that.

So I went back to IBC at mid-term that year.

The first thing I learned upon my arrival back at school was that Jerry's belief that the Lord wanted us together had not been dampened one bit. In fact, the night before I was due in, he was outside talking to some friends, and someone asked him why he was so happy. His answer was one of the first things I was told as I arrived back on campus: "My inspiration arrives tomorrow," he said.

Barbara Conner was my roommate all three years at IBC. She was also the pianist for the male quartet, and Jerry was the tenor for the quartet that year. Since Barbara was their pianist and I was her roommate, many times when the quartet had a singing engagement in the San Antonio area, I went along.

Coming back from one of those singing engagements in late May that year, we were all laughing, talking, singing and generally having a good time. All the rest of the fellows had their wives or dates with them. Since Jerry and I were the only people who were unattached, we wound up together. It was a soft, warm night—perfect for serenades and falling in love.

We stopped at a restaurant on the way home, and somewhere in the progress of that evening, I decided that Jerry Witt was one of the nicest young men I knew anywhere and that I enjoyed his company better than that of any other fellow on campus. It was too bad he was younger than me!

When we arrived back on campus, I told them all goodnight and went to my room, as it was getting late and I had lots I wanted to do before "lights out." Barbara was engaged to be married and therefore was allowed to talk to her fiancé, David, as long as she wanted but had to be in her room before 10 p.m. That night after going to the dorm, I noticed that Barbara wasn't around but assumed she was with David. Ten minutes before lights out, Barbara came running in. I started talking immediately about the service at the church where the quartet had sung, not noticing that she was in a serious frame of mind. This went on for a few minutes until Barbara looked at me sternly and said, "Nola Jean, do you know where I've been?"

"No," I said. "I knew you weren't in the dorm, but I assumed you were with David."

"Well, I wasn't," she said.

Since it seemed she wanted me to ask her where she had been, I did.

"Well, where have you been?"

"I've been out on the volleyball court all this time talking with Jerry," she continued. "About you!"

For once, I had no quick answer. All I said, was "Oh!"

"Do you know what he told me, Nola Jean? He said that he knows some day he will hold you in his arms and you will laugh together about all this but that right now, it is tearing him apart."

That's the night it began to dawn on me that maybe this thing was more than just a teenager's crush.

Although Jerry was still young, he was far ahead of his peers in spiritual matters. By this time in his life, he knew the Lord wanted him in full-time ministry. He studied his Bible constantly and often in the wee hours of the night would slip down to one of the classrooms or the chapel to be alone with God. Sometimes when he was surrounded by English-speaking people, he would pray in Spanish, feeling that the conversation was just between him and God.

One time, Jerry asked his friend Paul Dodge to go for a drive with him. Jerry wanted to show Paul a beehive full of honey that he found. So they got into Jerry's car and drove about fifteen or twenty miles out of town and down several small farm roads. They parked the car on a hill, got out and walked about half a mile looking for that beehive. They never found it. Finally, Paul looked at Jerry and asked, "How in the world did you find a bee hive way out here, anyway?"

Then Jerry told him the story about how he was out there one morning praying and heard these bees buzzing. As he began to investigate, he found their hive and decided to get Paul to go back with him so they could try to get the honey. It was one of those times when no one knew he slipped off alone and gone twenty or thirty miles just to be with the Lord in the early morning.

During this spring semester of my second year at IBC, I was

constantly amazed at the difference in Jerry, but still not quite amazed enough to give in on the romance question. Jerry was more insistent in his belief that God wanted us together, and I was beginning to waver in my firmness because the situation with my 'steady' in the Marines was gradually falling apart.

One night just before school was out that year, I was at the Administration Building talking with Jerry. By this time, we had become good friends and discussed things freely. Since the problem with my 'steady' was weighing heavily on my mind and since I needed to talk to someone about it, I talked to Jerry. I told him that I hadn't heard from the fellow in almost two months and that I really didn't know what to do about it. Jerry never tried to talk me into dropping the other fellow. He just kept himself and his affection before me all the time.

"Don't do anything about it," he said. "Leave it all in the hands of the Lord and let Him do what must be done. Besides," he said with that big smile of his, "I believe the Lord is saving you for me."

******

When I went back to IBC for my third and final year, things had changed. My Marine 'steady' had written, saying that he felt the Lord wanted us to break up. I was hurt, but not fatally. It had been a long time since we had seen each other, and my life was beginning to take a different direction than his. Also, Jerry was in college now, not high school. He was more attractive, more spiritual and more determined than ever in his pursuit of me. And I was ready to pay attention.

Jerry had had girlfriends, but none of them were serious, and when I got back to campus that fall, I began to let Jerry know that if he still meant all those wild things he'd been saying about me, I was interested in hearing more. We began to date on a steady basis.

IBC had some strict rules, and because we had started dating after school started, we were not allowed any special privileges. Even to be seen talking to each other on campus without permission could get us in trouble. Before we began dating, we could

20

talk together as much as we wanted. But once that line that separates friends from a courting couple had been crossed, we had to adhere to the courtship rules.

One day as we stood talking to each other during lunch break, we kept the width of the sidewalk between us. But, in spite of that, one of the faculty members came up to us with a super-serious countenance and said: "I've been watching you for some time, and you two haven't stopped talking for at least the past ten minutes. Now, Jerry, you go on down to the boys' dorm, and Nola Jean, you go to the girls' dorm, and you two break up this coupling off.

We couldn't have felt guiltier if we'd been caught in a clinch.

There was opposition from several people on campus because of the difference in our ages, and although that difference did make me hesitate at least once, now I was so far gone that all I could see was Jesus, Jerry and Mexico. As I played the piano during chapel services, I looked through the open lid of the Baby Grand straight into Jerry's eyes and sang, "If Jesus goes with me, I'll go—anywhere!" What I was really singing was, "If Jerry goes with me, I'll go anywhere!" We were in love. The first time for both of us.

Several years later, Jerry was telling a pastor friend of ours about our courtship and how he knew he wanted to marry me the minute we met, and the man literally sat there with his mouth open.

He said, "You mean to tell me that you were only fourteen years old when you met Nola, and you decided right then you wanted to marry her?"

Laughing, Jerry said, "That's right!"

The pastor shook his head and said, "Man, you were thinking about getting married at the age when I was still playing marbles."

Of course, it took me a lot longer to come to the same conclusion, but, yes, we were in love, and we wanted to get married. After all those years of holding out against Jerry's pursuit, when I finally did give in, I went into it with my whole heart. Jerry was my life, he was my hero, he was my love.

And that created a lot of trouble with my family. I was the

oldest child, and like all their other children, my mom and dad's pride and joy. I was ready to graduate from Bible College, and they had plans for me. They had spent thousands of dollars on music lessons for me. They had made big plans about what I would do at the church after I graduated, but here I was wanting to marry this young "whippersnapper" three years younger. But, horror of all horrors, that "whippersnapper" wanted to take me off to the wilds of Mexico.

We laughed about it in the years to come, but it was not funny at the time. My mom and dad were in agony, grieving over a daughter they felt certain was going to be wasted in Mexico. Jerry and I weren't getting any kicks out of insisting that we wanted to get married, either. It was a difficult time for all of us, a time of lots of tears, with conferences and talks that lasted until the wee hours of the morning.

I graduated from Bible College that year, and at our graduation, Pastor David Schoch gave me a prophetic word. The way it began frightened me. He said, "You have moved into a situation that has received lots of opposition from your friends and those around you. They have told you not to move into this thing, but you have chosen not to listen to them and have gone on with what you have felt you should do."

(By this time, my heart was palpitating, and I could hardly breathe. My thought was, O, God, have I missed you after all?)

Then Pastor Schoch went on: "But the way you have chosen is the way of the cross. I have led you that way, and I will continue to lead you as you follow me."

He said, "There will come a time of darkness in your life. It will be a darkness so black and without hope that without the grace of God, you will be lost. But, because God is with you, you will overcome, and, in that darkness, songs will be born."

After graduation, Jerry's parents wanted him to go back to Mexico with them, and my mom and dad wanted me to go back to Georgia with them. What we wanted was to be together, but it didn't seem like it was going to be like that right then. So we said goodbye and went home with our respective parents.

We were both miserable. I went ahead and got a job—and lost

ten pounds in two weeks. I was physically sick from missing Jerry so much. The letters I received from Jerry let me know that he was in the same condition. He was so skinny he couldn't afford to lose much weight or he'd be in the hospital. He wrote me nearly every day, and the only thing he was waiting for was his dad to return from a trip so he could talk to him about going to Georgia to be with me. When his dad got back, he was tired, it was late at night, and he didn't take Jerry seriously. By the next day, Jerry had pawned everything he owned (except his car) and was on his way to Georgia to get Nola Jean.

We were separated for about four weeks, and then one morning as I got to work, the telephone on my desk was ringing. When I picked it up, I heard Jerry's voice. Of all the incredible things, he was downstairs. I had given him my address at work as well as my home address, and he was so miserable that he had spent two hours that morning before I got to work finding the address of the office building where I worked. He wanted to see me as soon as I arrived that day instead of waiting until I went home in the afternoon.

It was a glorious reunion. We drove around north Georgia all day and went home that evening to my mom and dad's.

My parents were terrific. I know they were hurting and didn't want me to marry this young "Casanova" who had stolen my heart and was going to take me off to Mexico, but they did great. Jerry and I realized even then that my parents were suffering, and because of that, we did not behave with a spirit of rebellion. We continued to talk with my parents, and finally, they said, "Okay." Mom and Dad realized that we were not going to get married against their wishes, that we were willing to obey them, but they saw also how much we wanted to be together.

On July 1, 1959, we were married. My maternal grandfather, Pastor W. L. Cole, officiated. My grandfather wouldn't agree to perform the ceremony until he was certain my dad had said it was okay.

My dad marched down the church aisle with me and gave me away. From that day on, my mom and dad loved Jerry as their own son.

THE FOOLISHNESS OF GOD

****

The light was a source of encouragement beckoning me to the surface as I fought my way through an endless maze of smothering fog. Soon the fog became thinner and was penetrated by unbearable pain in my left arm. In my stupor, I fought the pain by trying to pull its source out of my arm, but every time I reached over to try to take the pain away, someone would catch my hand and hold it, keeping me from getting to the source of the pain. Even as my mind cried out against such treatment, I felt myself slipping and then drifting back into the fog.

The next time I woke, my arm was not aching so badly, and as I began to realize where I was, my eyes moved from the nurse who had been beside my bed all night to the blood that was being transfused into my body through my left arm—the source of the pain. My eyes fell on the apparatus standing next to my bed, which was slowly dripping the blood into my body, and my first thought was, *Except for the Lord, I would have died.*

It was the wee hours of the morning, May 11, 1960. Our first baby was born the night before. The delivery was long and complicated; the baby was a big boy, 9 pounds, 2 ounces and 22 inches long. Later I learned that Jerry had stood at the foot of my bed that night and cried out to God as the doctor and the nurse worked over me trying to get my blood pressure high enough to register on the sphygmomanometer. Finally, they were successful, and after the transfusion was started, I was doing better and things began to calm down.

Early the next morning, Jerry was back at the hospital. While we'd been waiting for the baby, I had insisted that I wanted to name the baby Jerry if it was a boy.

"No way," Jerry always said. "No son of mine is going to be called Junior."

But this morning when Jerry came back and saw that I was on the road to recovery and that the baby was a fine healthy child, he said: "After what you went through yesterday bringing that child into the world, you deserve to name him anything you want. As far as I am concerned, you could name him Herkimer if you want."

We named him Jerry Douglas Witt II.

****

Six weeks after the baby's birth, we left San Antonio for the summer to take advantage of Jerry's vacation from Bible school classes. Having scheduled missionary services in different churches that had shown an interest in our going to Mexico, we left San Antonio around midnight and headed for Fort Worth. The night was cool and clear. The stars shown brilliantly, our baby was asleep in his little bed in the back seat, and we were rejoicing in the fact that we were beginning the ministry the Lord had given us. We sang, we talked, and we praised God all the way from San Antonio to Fort Worth. It was like Jerry had written me two years earlier: "I've never been so happy in my life, and I know the reason is because we're in His perfect will. There's no joy outside it."

God blessed enormously in our travels that summer, so much so that Jerry began to think maybe he wouldn't go back to Bible school. Surely with the Lord blessing so much we should just go ahead and move into the ministry.

So he began to look at tents and other kinds of evangelistic equipment. He bought a tent and set it up for a revival meeting in a small town in central Georgia. Some of the people from my dad's church drove down for the night services, and local residents responded well also. Jerry felt certain this was another sign that God wanted him to forget about Bible school and move into active ministry.

One afternoon, a windstorm with some rain came. It didn't seem like a big deal, but about thirty minutes after it passed over, we got a telephone call from some people who had their business near the place where the tent was located. They told us the tent was laying flat on the ground.

Jerry jumped into the car and went screeching up there to see if it were true. That tent was down, with the poles and lights scattered all over the place. The piano and the folding chairs were all right, but the tent was destroyed. That revival meeting came to a quick halt.

We were hurt and confused. We still owed money on that tent. Couldn't God see that we were trying to serve him? But, before the day was over, Jerry spent time alone with God, and that night, as I was putting the baby to bed, he told me he was beginning to feel that the entire episode had been the hand of God.

Startled, I looked at him and asked, "How on earth could that have been the hand of the Lord? We owed money on that tent, and now it's gone."

He said, "I know. But I am beginning to think that I missed God. I believe this is the Lord letting me know that I don't need to get caught up in any revival meetings or evangelistic work. He wants me concentrating on Mexico, and He wants me to go back to Bible College for that final year of study. He destroyed what I was putting my hopes in and left me with no choice. We're going back to San Antonio, and I am finishing school."

Back in San Antonio, Jerry and I both held down full-time jobs. He was keeping up with his schoolwork as well. At one job, he was working seven days a week, and he was drinking fifteen to sixteen cups of coffee each day just trying to stay on his feet. At the same time, our baby was growing up and calling a friend of ours "daddy."

During Christmas vacation of his senior year, several of the students from IBC made a trip down to visit some mission works in Mexico. We scrapped the money together and went along. We visited La Nueva Esperanza Bible School, just south of Monterrey. When the director of the Bible school learned that Jerry spoke Spanish and that he was looking for an opening for ministry in Mexico, he invited him down to work with them in the school. Jerry wanted to go right then, and the director wanted him to go immediately. During the few days that we were at the school, we were in several services, visited with some of the students and saw some of the need for missionaries in Mexico. As Jerry spoke with the people and attended the services, he wept. He wept nearly the entire time we were there. When we arrived back in San Antonio, he decided he wanted to go to Mexico. Now. None of that graduating from Bible school nonsense. The need was current, he was able to take care of the need, and he wanted to go now.

I began to pray. I felt he should finish school. But Jerry insisted that we should prepare to leave. I gave my two-week notice at my job and began to try to prepare myself psychologically for the move. But somehow everything worked out, and Jerry decided to finish school. He did finally graduate in May that year. When he marched down the aisle and received his diploma, some of us felt that a major battle had been won.

Immediately following graduation, our family started out on a trip that lasted a year. We traveled from Texas to Georgia to Florida to Indiana to Illinois to Arkansas to Kansas and finally stopped for a while in California, where Jerry's parents lived. Throughout all the travels, one door after another opened for ministry, and we had no problem staying busy. However, once we reached California, it was like the Lord stopped all movement, and the doors for ministry closed.

So Jerry began looking for work. Again, everything he tried was stopped. Either he couldn't find work, or something would happen so he couldn't get to the place where the work was located. On one of those efforts we thought there might be some work in central California, but as we left to go there, one of the brakes on our car caught fire and burned out. We couldn't get it fixed in time to make the trip, so we borrowed Jerry's grandmother's car and drove up, only to have the generator on that car go out. No work was found, either.

A couple of days later, we were back at his grandmother's house, and Jerry decided to go down to Southern California, where his dad was working. Once again, we loaded our family in the car and set out looking for work. This time we were traveling into the face of fifty- to sixty-mile-per-hour winds, pulling a trailer uphill. The car couldn't handle it, so the transmission overheated, the oil boiled over, and smoke came out as if coming from a bonfire Once again, we returned to Jerry's grandmother's.

When we finally gave up on the idea of finding work, a friend of ours from Northern California contacted us and helped us schedule several services in his area and we were once again "in the flow" and on our way to Mexico. A man in that area of

California gave us an old truck that he thought would be of use in Mexico, and when we left California heading south again, we were towing that truck behind our car. The first thing that happened on that trip was that the tow bar snapped, and the truck had to be driven. Now we had two vehicles to drive instead of one. There had been a gasoline war in Southern California when we were preparing to leave, so Jerry bought two fifty-gallon drums of gasoline, and we carried it on the back of the truck all the way to the Mexican border, using the gasoline as we moved along on the trip.

Of course, there was little money, and that truck kept giving us trouble across Arizona and New Mexico. Somewhere near Deming, New Mexico, the right rear tire on the truck blew out. Jerry fixed it, got into the truck again, and, four miles later, the tire blew again. This time he had to take the tire to a place in Deming to get it fixed, and by the time he got back to where he had left the truck, it was dark and 20 degrees outside. I'd been listening to the news on the car radio all day. They had been forecasting a big winter storm, and we were in the middle of it.

We thought we would just keep driving so we could stay warm (we didn't have money for a hotel room), but then we discovered that the truck's lights didn't work, so we had to stop whether we wanted to or not.

That night remains in my memory as one of the longest and coldest nights of my life. We had to stay in the car because we had no money and no credit cards for a hotel room. That night we used one-fourth of a tank of gasoline just running the car's heater, trying to stay warm. The only one who was comfortable was Little Jerry. I had wrapped him up in a couple of blankets, and he slept the entire night. Jerry and I were glad to see the sun the next morning.

Somewhere on this trip, even before we arrived in California, we discovered that our second child was on the way. So when we left California, instead of heading straight to Mexico, we went back to San Antonio, where we waited for that child to be born.

God was continuing to bless us, and after we got back to Texas, several doors for ministry opened, and people continued to show an interest in the work in Mexico. It was during this "waiting period" that Jerry took his flight instruction, and some pastors in the area helped him buy his first airplane.

On May 19, 1962, Jonathan Mark Witt was born. He was a beautiful child, in command from the moment he made his first appearance. In the hospital delivery room, the nurse turned Mark around so I could see him. He already had quit crying, and as she turned him, he looked me square in the eyes as though to say, "Don't worry. I've got everything under control."

Jerry had his airplane, our waited-for baby had been born, and different churches and pastors were committing themselves to help us with the vision for Mexico. We were excited because we could see that the time for our moving into Mexico was getting closer and closer.

2

"Here We Are, You Lucky People"

One of Jerry's closest friends was John Eils, also a missionary to Mexico. Jerry and John lived together in Mexico before our marriage and were involved in several "situations" that only adult men who love a joke could have been a part of. John came to San Antonio just a few days after Mark was born and wanted Jerry to take his little Piper Super Cruiser plane down to the area where he was working in the state of Tamaulipas and do some evangelism. Jerry, always ready for another flight in his airplane, agreed quite readily to make the trip. After all, he couldn't move his family into Mexico just yet because Mark was too small, and what better way to mark the time than to make a trip to Mexico himself. So John and Jerry flew to Mexico.

Just after John and Jerry left, I had a dream. In this dream, I saw the plane come down in a forced landing, and although John and Jerry were okay, the plane had a good deal of damage.

The night before John and Jerry were due back into San Antonio, I went to church. Right away someone came up to me and asked: "How are Jerry and John? Are they all right?"

"I suppose they're all right," I replied. "Since we don't have a telephone at our apartment, I haven't heard anything from them directly since they left."

"Oh," this person said. "Then you haven't heard?"

"Haven't heard what?" I asked.

"Well, maybe I shouldn't be telling you this, but I heard a

30

rumor that they had crashed!"

At first I was panic-stricken. But then common sense took over. I calmed down, had a talk with the pastor and realized that my dream was true. Jerry and John had called the church. They had crashed, but they were both okay.

John and Jerry were flying at a low altitude over a remote village and dropping Gospels of St. John out the window.[3] Since John had more experience with this kind of flying, he was flying the plane, and Jerry was in the back seat throwing out the Gospels. They had been flying for a couple of hours and were beginning to tire, so they decided to land the plane. There was no emergency or need to land. They were simply tired and wanted to rest a while before finishing that day's work.

As they looked around for a place to land, they spotted a small dirt air strip off to one side and decided that was where they would land the plane.

John was still flying, and as they made the approach to the little strip, Jerry was looking over John's shoulder at the gauges on the plane. John was not as familiar with the plane as Jerry, so when Jerry began to feel that they were not maintaining the proper air speed for the altitude they were holding, Jerry shouted: "John!"

But it was too late.

The plane dropped fifty feet out of the air and slammed onto the dirt strip. The landing gear collapsed, and as they slid several hundred feet, Jerry and John were thrown around and the cabin filled with dust and debris. It seemed like a long time before the plane finally came to a stop. The little Super Cruiser came to a halt and tilted up on its nose with the propeller bent around the engine cone.

Their first thought was, Fire!, so they scrambled hurriedly out of the plane. Their next thought was that they were both all right, but that the plane was in terrible condition. They grieved over that little airplane.

It wasn't but a few minutes until the police arrived. Because it was an American airplane, with two American pilots, and it landed on a remote dirt strip, they were suspected of smuggling. The federal aviation inspector came to the site and ordered that they be held for investigation.

They were taken to the nearest large city, where they were first placed in jail and later moved to a hotel where they were held under house arrest until the matter could be cleared up. It took a couple of days, but they were cleared and able to make their way back to San Antonio, but with the little airplane on the back of a flat-bed truck.

Jerry said later, "We didn't even have the privilege of being able to say that we were thrown into jail because of preaching the Gospel. We were thrown into jail because they thought we were smugglers."

The plane was eventually fixed, but it was never the same.

Soon after Jerry returned from that trip, Mark and I were released by the doctor, and we were finally able to begin the move to Mexico. We loaded everything we owned into a house trailer and began the trip. We were using an old carry-all[4] that another man had given us to pull the trailer with because we'd sold the car. We still owed money on the car and didn't want to go to Mexico with debts, so we sold it and were using this carry-all (which really belonged in the junk pile) to pull the trailer to Mexico. Thirteen miles out of San Antonio, we had to call a friend to come and get us because the carry-all simply would not pull the trailer.

Jerry called Paul Bostow.

"Paul," he said. "We're thirteen miles out of town, and the carry-all can't pull this trailer. The generator has already gone out, the seal on the differential gear is going out, and we've already used half a tank of gas and three quarts of oil. We're not going to be able to make it."

Paul came for us, and our excitement about finally leaving for Mexico turned into disappointment as we had to spend still a few more days in San Antonio before the details were worked out and we were able to leave again.

Paul decided to pull the trailer for us to Monterrey with his own truck, and we would just travel in the carry-all with the children. This was a tremendous blessing and an answer to prayer.

Still the problems had not finished. Fifty miles south of San Antonio, the trailer blew a tire. That was just the beginning of that episode. We got that tire fixed, and just before we arrived in Laredo, Texas (on the border), the trailer blew another tire. Jerry spent his last $40 buying two tires for the trailer.

When we finally got through Mexican customs, it was exciting. As we turned onto the highway that would lead us to Monterrey, Jerry turned to me with a big grin and asked, "Do you realize where we are?"

Yes, we were finally in Mexico, across the border with our two children and all our earthly belongings, on our way to Durango, where we were planning to live and minister for a few years and then move to another area.

In Monterrey, some other friends loaded our things into their little trailer (so the big heavy trailer could be taken back to San Antonio), and they drove us down to Durango. We found a house and moved into it the same day.

While we were looking for a house in Durango, Little Jerry (who was two years old), decided to follow his dad and our friend on one of their errands. Because of the excitement of finally being in Durango and finding a house, we didn't even realize he was gone for at least thirty minutes. When we realized he had disappeared, everyone sprang into immediate action. Our friend went in one direction, his wife in another, and Jerry in yet another direction looking for the little guy. It had happened near a plaza, and I was walking the floor in that plaza with Mark in my arms, praying desperately for God to help us find our little boy.

"God, what is this?" I cried out. "I haven't even been in this city for twenty-four hours, and already my child has disappeared."

I cried, I begged, I prayed, I pleaded with God to help us find that little bundle of humanity.

Suddenly, I heard a shout, and there on the corner stood our friend with Little Jerry in his arms. He'd found him already loaded into the car of some people who had found him standing on the street corner looking lost. They said they were taking him to the police station.

"He doesn't talk much, does he?" the man who found him commented. "I asked him his name, I asked him where his parents were, and all I could get him to say was 'gum'!"

Of course, he doesn't talk much, I thought to myself. He's only two years old, and besides, he doesn't know Spanish.

Altogether, Little Jerry was away from us for a little more than an hour. When our friend found him, he was hanging out the window of the car in which he had been placed yelling at our friend and waving his arms. He was ready for someone to find him.

Actually, Little Jerry had been a wanderer since the day he learned to walk. He'd go over to the neighbor's house to play with their dog or just go strolling down the street to see what he could find. I think he was cured that day. He never did any more wandering.

*****

The day after our arrival in Durango, Jerry sat down at our old, battered typewriter and wrote the following newsletter to our friends:

> *Yesterday, rain clouds hovered over the city of Durango, Mexico, as we approached. Today it has been raining lightly, and the farmers are in anticipation of heavy rains. Usually, we would pay little attention to rain, but this time, we feel it has a real significance. You see, not only has Mexico been suffering from the lack of natural rain for several years, but it has also seen little or no spiritual rain. For this reason, as Nola and I entered the city answering the call of the Lord, our hearts cried out for a real downpour from heaven for these people.*

*****

We had worked so long and so hard preparing for our time in Mexico. We had traveled, we had prayed, we had bought equipment, raised support, had two babies, and finally we were actually in the country. Including the years we were in Bible school, we spent at least five years preparing for that move, and all the time we were preparing, there was a feeling of urgency; a feeling that time was running out and that we needed to get to the land of our calling and get on with the work God had given us to do. Our entire lives had been focused on getting to Mexico, and because of all the concentration and intensity that had gone into getting us there, I felt that the Mexican people would be waiting for us with open arms. Jerry didn't share my hope because he had lived in Mexico for five years as an adolescent, but I wanted to announce on every street corner, "All right, you lucky people. We are here! You can come and get the Gospel now!"

Of course, that doesn't even faintly resemble what really happened.

Our vision was always to raise up congregations in places where there were no evangelical congregations and to establish a Bible school for the training of national leadership. We didn't want to go to places that already had a Gospel witness, and we didn't want to work in an already established church. The vision was to go into the unreached areas of the state of Durango. The Bible school would take several years to develop, but we began immediately to look around and see where a church was needed. We found several little towns in the Durango City area and began to go into these places to evangelize and hold services.

But nearly every place we went during those early days, they threw us out.

One of the places we went to was a little town named Carrillo Puerto. We had the name and address of a man in that village who had written asking for a correspondence course on the Life of Christ. The first time Jerry went in and looked up this man, he was received with open arms. The people were happy to see him, and they were anxious to hear more about the Gospel. The first service was scheduled for the following Sunday. When he and a Mexican pastor who was to help with the service flew over Carrillo Puerto that Sunday for the service, they could see that there was a crowd of more than 300 people waiting for them.

Jerry thought it was because the people were so happy about their coming that they had formed a reception committee to give them a good welcome.

"Praise God," he said as he turned to the Mexican pastor. "It looks like we're going to have a good crowd today!"

It was a reception committee all right, but not of the kind that gives good welcomes. About five people of that 300 were causing trouble. They had sticks and machetes in their hands and were yelling at the evangelicals to get out of their town.

"We don't need you or want you," they shouted. "We're already Christians, so just get out of here and stay out."

Jerry and the Mexican pastor didn't give up that easily but tried to reason with the people and talk with them. Nothing did any good.

Suddenly, one of the trouble-makers shouted, "Where's a match? Give me a match. We'll set this airplane on fire, and that will get rid of them for good."

Well, a burned-out airplane was the last thing he wanted, so Jerry and those who were trying to hold the service decided it would be best to leave and come back another time. Still, there were people on the ground who wanted to hear what the evangelicals had to say, and they stretched out their hands to receive the Gospels of St. John that Jerry gave to them. As Jerry turned to get back into the plane after all the yelling and trouble, an old man was standing beside the plane with tears running down his face. He told Jerry he was so disappointed at the way things had turned out. Others around him were weeping also.

They did return to that village in a ground vehicle so as not to attract so much attention. But the trouble-makers kept coming. On one occasion, the uproar was so bad that the district mayor sent army troops in to keep order. The people were told that Mexico is a free country and if these evangelicals want to hold their services, they could do so. Still, no church was ever established in that village.

Another village was only a few minutes out of the city of Durango. It was called El Conejo (the Rabbit), and was a desolate, rocky place. The entire village was built out of rocks: the little streets, the walls, the houses. When we first began going into El Conejo, we had a good reception. The people were hungry to hear the Word of God, and they came out in good numbers to hear the preaching. We'd heard rumors about some people trying to cause trouble, but the response had been so positive that we didn't think anything bad would happen.

Then one night, our friend Daniel Gutierrez was preaching in that village. People were sitting at the entrance to the lady's house where the services were being held, they were standing all around the room and even on the outside trying to hear the message that night. It was exciting. Finally, we were seeing something positive happen as a result of our being in Mexico.

At one point in the service, I saw a man get Jerry and take him outside. As it turned out, he came and got Jerry because some men were letting the air out of the tires on our carry-all. So Jerry went out and sat on the hood of the vehicle to keep an eye on everything and at the same time to witness and talk with the men who were gathered around. When the service was finished, the lady whose house the services were held at was worried. She tried to get Jerry to move the carry-all into her corral and all of us to spend the night there because she had heard rumors about what some of the people in the village were planning to do to us that night—and it wasn't good. So she wanted us to wait until the morning to leave. We didn't feel that we wanted to do that, so she asked Jerry to at least let me and the two children stay with her because she was worried. When Jerry told me what she was saying, I said "No way!" I didn't want to stay in that place with my two children unless Jerry was staying, too.

Having decided to drive the ten miles back to Durango, our family and that of Pastor Daniel climbed into the carry-all for the trip back to town. Jerry put the women and children in the back of the carry-all because he figured that any violence would be aimed at the front of the vehicle.

As we began to pull out from in front of the lady's house, we had to move slowly because the narrow street was made of rocks—and not smooth rock pavement, either. It was made of rocks of different sizes with every rock having a different surface and a point that stuck up out of the ground. The village of El Conejo is built on a rocky mountainside, and I think the streets were just places where they had left the rocks that were already there and tried to fill them in with dirt. The carry-all had what they call a "grandma," or a super-low gear. That means it can pull much lower than the normal gear box. Jerry put the carry-all in "grandma" and began to move slowly from in front of the lady's house. As he began to move the vehicle, the lady walked along beside the vehicle. Stopping the truck, Jerry asked her, "What are you doing?"

"I'm going with you," she said. "I'm going with you to the outskirts of town to make sure you get out all right."

Jerry said, "If you're going with us, get inside the carry-all. Don't walk outside."

So she jumped up into the right front seat and shouted, "Vamonos!" ("Let's go!")

As soon as possible, Jerry moved out of the "grandma" gear and into first.

Still, that wasn't fast enough to suit the lady, so she shouted again, "Vamonos!"

She shouted that word three times before we were going fast enough to please her.

As she kept shouting "Vamonos!," the carry-all began to rock all over those narrow streets with its lights flashing against the sky and then against the ten-foot-tall rocky walls in front of us. We were fast approaching an intersection of another little street just like the first one. I knew we were going to have to make a sharp turn to the right, or else we would crash head on into the rock wall that was built on that street also. As we approached that intersection, Jerry shouted, "Hang on everybody!"

And hang on we did. I remember thinking we would not be able to make it, we were going to crash into that wall. We were bouncing all over the back of the carry-all, but somehow, with the help of the Lord, Jerry swung the carry-all around that sharp corner and kept it on the street. As we turned the first corner, we found the first pile of rocks. They had been piled across the narrow street a couple of feet high in an effort to force us to stop and then the mob would have us at their mercy.

The lady took one look at the rocks and shouted, "Don't stop! They're waiting for us!" So Jerry didn't stop but knocked those rocks everywhere as he took the carry-all through as fast as he could.

Before we got out of that village and back up on the highway to Durango, we ran through four piles of rocks like that. We saw the people with their piles of rocks beside them to stone us. We even received a few blows from some rocks they did throw at us, but God was with us that night. Even the men letting the air out of the tires proved to be a blessing. Not one tire blew as Jerry plowed through those rock piles, and it was because about half of the air normally carried in the tires was gone. The carry-all was sold a few months later for junk, but that night, it was exactly what was needed to deliver us from the "snare of the enemy."

Out on the highway again, Jerry stopped the carry-all to let the lady who had accompanied us get out and go back home. When we stopped, she looked at him and asked, "What are you doing?"

"Stopping," he said, "so you can get out and go back home."

"Absolutely not," she said. "Those people know I came out with you, and they know you held the services in my home. I'm going into the city with you and spending several days with a friend of mine, and then I'll go back home in open daylight."

We tried several times and ways after that incident to get into that village with the Gospel, but today, thirty-five years after all that happened, there is still no Gospel witness in the town of El Conejo.

Not only was there persecution and opposition everywhere we went, we were encountering problems in other areas of our lives as well.

The two boys were sick all the time. Little Jerry was able to throw off the innumerable stomach infections so dominant in the Third World better than the baby because he was older. Even at that, he managed to fall one day and had stitches in his upper lip, where he has a scar to this very day.

But Mark was the child that nearly died from all the stomach problems. In spite of the fact that I boiled everything that went into his mouth—even the spoon I fed him with—he came down with one stomach problem after another. (One doctor told me the bacteria was in the air we breathed.) At six months of age, Mark only weighed twelve pounds and in some ways resembled a shriveled up little old man more than he did a baby. But we kept battling, and after about a year, he began to have longer spaces of time between the sicknesses. He began to put on weight and look more like a child of his age should look.

During the first six months of our time in Mexico, our children were sick and we were being run out of every place we tried to enter with the Gospel. On top of that, the financial situation was bad.

We went to Mexico with the promise of help from numerous pastors and friends. One of the first lessons we learned is that promises are sometimes not kept. We had no furniture, not even a table on which to eat. Jerry and I sat on folding chairs to eat, and we had to feed Little Jerry as he sat on the floor—there weren't enough folding chairs for him. We went weeks without meat of any kind. That's when I learned about meat substitutes. The lights were turned off. There was no gasoline for the vehicle or the airplane. An old bed had been given to us when we left San Antonio, and every night, we had to prop it up again because it kept falling in. One night after Jerry had fixed it for the third time, he finally said, "Leave it. We'll just sleep on the mattress on the floor."

Yes, there were times when we wondered what on earth we were doing in that place. But through it all, God was faithful, and our belief that God had really brought us to this place became more and more certain. We looked for more places in which to minister where we wouldn't be rejected, we fought the diseases that our children contracted with such regularity, and we asked God to give us the strength to remain faithful in the face of seemingly unending financial problems. We went several weeks during one of those times when the only thing we had to eat was zucchini squash with macaroni and cheese. Sometimes Jerry even walked the eight-mile round trip to the airport to see about the airplane because there was no money for gasoline, buses or taxis.

But one day, everything ran out. There was no money to buy squash, macaroni and cheese, or even baby formula. There was no money for gasoline for the vehicle. We were quite literally at the bottom of the barrel. I gave my two-month-old baby his last bottle at the same time that Jerry left walking to go to the post office. I gave Little Jerry something for breakfast, and the boys settled down for a nap while we waited to see what would happen next.

It seemed to me that Jerry was taking an awfully long time to go to the post office, even for walking. Four hours later, Mark was beginning to get restless and was looking for that next bottle. I was beginning to get worried. But about the time the situation was becoming critical, especially for the baby, who wanted his meals on time, there was a knock on the door.

I ran to open the door, and there stood Jerry with a big grin on his face and a box of groceries in his arms. He had walked to the post office, found a letter with a $10 check inside, walked to the grocery store and then walked home with the necessary food to get us through another few days.

We learned several lessons during that time of living from day to day. One valuable thing we learned was that even the smallest of offerings could be what was needed to feed our family. That was what was needed for right then. God would take care of what was to be needed for the next day.

Also, we learned that other people had the same sort of problems. Another time when the finances were low (we had about $5 to our name), we decided to go to Daniel and Dolores Gutierrez's home for a visit and cheer ourselves up. When we got there, we found them in even worse condition than us. They also had a little boy who had to have milk, and they had none, nor money to buy milk. So we took the last $5 we had, bought their baby some milk and a few small items to make a meal, and we all ate together and had a great time of fellowship. The next day, God sent in some more money, and we were able to keep going.

Those first six months were the worst in every way. There was more persecution, there were more financial problems, and there was more sickness. It was almost like we were being tried by fire, and once we passed that level of the test, we moved on to another test. Of course, we had other financial problems in the years to come as well as other health problems. There were also more times of opposition, but there was never a time when all of these things were happening at the same time with the same intensity as they did during those first six months.

But we were settling in. We bought our first pieces of furniture. We found some villages where the people did want to hear the Gospel. The children began to adapt to the climate and the food. By the end of the first year of our time in Mexico, Jerry was flying into some ten villages each week and preaching the Gospel to people who had never heard it, and the people were responding. We had been able to buy a piece of land on the outskirts of Durango on which we planned to build the Bible school. God was opening doors and blessing. Durango was beginning to feel like home.

In spite of all the opposition and problems, we also had a lot of fun. One of the most encouraging things about those first few months was the way the missionaries from other denominations who lived in the city of Durango rallied around us and helped to encourage us and keep us going. There were Methodist missionaries, Reformed Mennonite missionaries and Southern Baptist missionaries.

Baptist missionaries Gilbert and Carolyn Ross had children about the age of our boys, so we saw quite a bit of them. Also, Gilbert was interested in the flying aspect of missions, and he and Jerry spent a good deal of time together flying into different villages that needed the Gospel. They also spent some time together in friendship, making some hunting trips back up into the mountains.

But they never got anything. During that first year we were in Mexico, in the month of December (it was cold and raining), Gilbert and Jerry decided to go fishing instead of hunting. They took a homemade pontoon boat out onto the lake. The only problem was that the boat leaked, and as they sat out on the lake that afternoon fishing, they suddenly found themselves standing in water with the boat under their feet.

As Gilbert was describing the episode, he laughed and said, "That was fine for Jerry to be standing in that water because it only came to his chest. But I was treading water."

Jerry was 6'3" tall, and Gilbert was about 5'6" tall.

At least they came back with some fish.

One of the villages where we ministered on a regular basis was a little town named Paura de Mesquital. Paura was about forty miles up into the mountains on a difficult road, but the most interesting part was that we had to ford two rivers to get to Paura. But we were happy to be able to work with the people there, so fording those rivers was just another part of the adventure.

That is, it was an adventure until one cold day in December of that first year, when we returned from a Christmas service with the carry-all full of different members of my family who were visiting for the holidays. It had been an outstanding day, and we were on our way back home. But it was dark and cold now, and the river was high. There was some discussion as to whether we should attempt to cross the river, but what choice did we have? It was either cross it or sit on the side of the river in the cold with about ten people, including women and small children. So we decided to cross the river.

Usually, the carry-all would take us through situations like this, but this time, it failed us. Right in the deepest part of the river with the water almost waist deep, the motor choked down and quit. There we were, with all these people in the carry-all, it was cold and dark, and water was coming into the cab of the vehicle. There was nothing to do but for the men to get out and try to push the carry-all out. Jerry, my dad, my brother and a Mexican brother all took their shoes off, rolled up their pants legs and stepped out into that December-cold water. That is, they all took their shoes off except my dad. He didn't even roll his pants legs up.

When Jerry told him that he needed to take his good shoes off or they would be ruined in all that water, my dad replied, "My feet are more valuable than these shoes. So I'll just ruin the shoes instead of ruining my feet trying to walk around on the rocky bottom of this river."

This was my parents' first visit to Mexico, and they loved it. Although they had been opposed to our marriage in the beginning, my parents became an integral part of the work in Mexico. You see, my dad had experienced a revolution in his spirit, and it changed his life and the life of his church forever. During the first few months after we were married, Jerry and my dad talked and argued about every phase of mission work imaginable. Jerry challenged my dad, my dad got defensive, and they were off in a big argument again. In one of those conversations, Jerry asked my dad why his church didn't believe in missions.

"Of course we believe in missions," my daddy responded.

"Then," asked Jerry, "why don't you give any money to missions?"

"We do give money to missions," my dad replied.

"How much money have you given to missions in the past month?" asked Jerry.

"Well, none."

"How much money have you given to missions in the past two months?"

"Well, none."

"How much money have you given to missions in the past six months?"

"None."

"All right," continued Jerry. "How much money have you given to missions during the past year?"

In his own words, my dad says he was glad they finally got to the one-year level because he was able to answer the question positively.

"We sent $10 last year to a missionary in Japan," my dad said.

"Besides," my dad continued, "we need to do missionary work here in the U.S. more than in some foreign country. Wait until we get our own country evangelized and then we can start on some of the other areas of the world. We don't want to send our money and people off to some remote part of the world when we still have needs here at home. After all, we want to keep this situation balanced."

"Pastor Holder," Jerry said. "I'd like for you to make an experiment for me. Beginning at your church and driving in any direction you choose for the distance of one mile, tell me how many churches you would have in that area."

"Well, I don't know how many, but there would be several," my dad answered.

Jerry said, "Until the mission fields of the world have the same access to the Gospel as the U.S. does, we cannot say there is no need and that we don't need to send missionaries and mission funds to these countries. That is the way to keep the balance—by seeing that those who have never heard have the opportunity to know about Jesus."

That night my dad agonized in his soul about the things Jerry had been telling him. Had he been wrong in not being involved in foreign missions? Was it true that the peoples in the foreign countries had as much need for the Gospel as those in the United States? Had he been narrow-minded in his approach to world evangelization? He didn't sleep much that night as he wrestled with these things in his spirit. Finally, around daybreak, there was a breakthrough.

"Oh, God," my dad cried out from the depths of his soul. "Forgive me, for I have been a selfish man. I have thought only of my own needs. Forgive me, and I'll change. Forgive me, Lord, and we'll make this church a missions-minded church."

More than thirty years later, that little church has sent out several missionaries as well as given hundreds of thousands of dollars in mission funds. My dad himself is approaching his eightieth birthday, and he still makes a trip down to Mexico at least once each year to minister and rejoice at what he, through the grace of God, has been involved with all these years. Of his own nine children, he has helped to send five of them to the mission field.

But this was their first trip to Mexico, and they enjoyed it. They waded in the cold river waters we forded at night, they rode in the back of the truck seated flat on the floor for hours as we went up into the mountains for different services, they walked miles on rocky paths as we made our way into another village, and they were amazed at the response of the people as they heard the Gospel for the first time. They became involved. They became a part of the Mexican people on that first trip, and they've been involved ever since.

Yes, we were settling in. Durango was becoming our home.

That first year in Mexico was also a time of constant discovery.

We discovered Mexican weddings. Mexican weddings are designed to be a witness to unsaved relatives, and they hold a full-fledged worship service with singing of hymns and choruses as well as a normal-sized sermon. Then, nearly every wedding I've attended in Mexico has started late. They always have to wait for the bride, or the couple, or the parents or someone. By the time they get started late, have at least a two-hour service and then go to the reception, where they serve food and play games, you know that you've been to a wedding.

My first wedding in Mexico started two hours late, had at least a two-hour service, and then another long meal and time of games. The wedding was scheduled to begin at noon, and at 9 p.m., when we left the reception, it was still going strong. And it makes sense. After all that effort and expense, why do something that is over within thirty minutes? I like Mexican weddings.

We discovered the innovative nature of the people who live in the Mexican villages. One night as we went to one of the villages for a house service, all during the service, we would keep hearing this "peep, peep," which sounded like it was coming from a small chicken. But there were no chickens to be seen. At the end of the service, we asked around and discovered that one of the ladies had a sick chicken near her bosom. It was sick and she was trying to nurse it back to health by keeping it next to her body.

In that village, I listened to one of the most incredible conversion testimonies I've ever heard.

It seems this woman was the ringleader of all opposition against the evangelicals in that little town. She didn't like the evangelicals, and she didn't want them around. She led demonstrations, she cat-called them when they were present and just generally did everything she could to cause trouble.

But one day, as she was walking back from the river near the village, a violent thunderstorm came suddenly. The wind was blowing hard, and the rain was coming down so hard she couldn't see where she was walking. She was knocked to the ground by a bolt of lightening. Her family came looking for her and found her stunned and unable to talk, lying in the middle of the muddy street.

By now, the storm had passed over, and they took her home and put her to bed. The doctor came and said she was stunned from this blow but that she probably would be all right. There were no burns on her body, just this inability to move around and talk.

She lay in bed for about two weeks, and during the entire time, God spoke to her. He told her that she had been wrong in opposing these people who had brought the Word of God to her village. He told her she needed to repent and accept the Lord Jesus Christ as her Savior.

When she finally got up out of her bed and resumed her life, she was a changed woman. She gave her heart to the Lord. She testified to her relatives and friends, and at the time I heard the testimony, she was one of the leaders in that small congregation.

Yes, we were feeling at home and enjoying the work God had given us to do.

A little more than a year after our arrival in Durango, our third son was born. Philip Andrew Witt weighed 9 pounds, $10\frac{1}{2}$ ounces. He was a blonde, with a smile as wide as the world. He was the happiest of all babies and could make anyone smile, regardless of how weighted down they might feel.

So Mark had to move out of the crib and make room for his baby brother. But we didn't have a bed for him, so we bedded him down in an old playpen—something else that had been given to us—and it was quite rickety. One night not long after we got back to Durango after Philip was born, we had put the boys to bed for the night when we heard a big crash and a deep-throated yowl. As we went running into the boys' room, we found Mark crawling out from under the wreckage of his playpen. The thing had finally collapsed. We went down the next day and bought him a bed.

Yes, we were feeling at home in Durango, but some aspects of the opposition and persecution continued to be a part of our daily life.

The most troublesome and repetitious of all the opposition and persecution was that which was connected to the airplane. With time, most of the other persecution began to calm down, but the threats concerning the airplane were continuous.

One day, a lady from one of the churches up in the mountains made the trip all the way into the city to find Jerry.

"Yesterday," she said, "the religious leader in my town came to my house with a message for you."

"What was the message?" Jerry asked.

"He said that I am to tell that American friend of mine that if you ever fly over his village again, they are going to shoot you down. Oh, Jerry, please don't fly over that area again. We don't want those people to really shoot you down."

Jerry assured her that he firmly believed that neither that leader nor anyone else could shoot him down or do him any bodily harm unless the Lord stepped aside and let them do it. He didn't discount the woman's warning, but he didn't feel he could allow things like that to paralyze him emotionally and make him afraid to do what he had come to Mexico to do. He felt that his life was in the Lord's hands, and if God felt He could get more glory from his death than from his life, then he was willing to die.

In March 1964, Jerry was flying from Monclova, Coahuila, back to Durango after a time in the United States raising money for the Bible school. At the end of that trip, he wrote: "When I sighted Durango over the nose of the plane, joy welled up inside me at seeing the place again, and once more I asked God to give us a fruitful ministry here. I know this is where God wants us."

The End of the Beginning

For Christmas that year, I gave Jerry a copy of the book *Jungle Pilot* by Russell Hitt. The story of five missionaries who were killed by the Auca Indians in Ecuador, South America, it is especially the story of the pilot, Nate Saint. Every day when Jerry came in from one of his trips, he disappeared into the back room and read some more of the story of this missionary pilot. On the day he finished the book, he was in the back room for a long time, and when he came out, I saw that he had been praying because the tears were still fresh on his face. He came to the door of the kitchen and stood watching me as I worked. Finally I looked up and asked, "Did you finish the book?"

"Yes," he said with a twisted smile. "It was great. What a glorious way to die." Pausing for a few seconds, he continued, "When it's my time to go, that's the way I want the Lord to take me."

"Do you mean you want to be killed by the Indians?" I asked.

"No," he said. "I mean I want to be giving out the Gospel when I die—in my airplane."

****

It had been a busy day, and now we had visitors. They were two ladies who worked with Intervarsity Fellowship in Mexico City, and they needed a place to spend the night. After eating supper, Jerry went into the back room to prepare for a flight he was making the next day. The children and I stayed in the kitchen/dining room talking with our visitors. As we sat around the table, Jerry came in and laid the aerial chart with which he was working on the table in front of me. Aerial charts are enlarged maps that pilots use to chart their courses. They show every river, canyon, mountain, town and even small settlements for navigational purposes.

"I want to show you exactly where I will be flying tomorrow," he said. Placing his finger on the map, he showed me the valley in the northern part of the state of Zacatecas where he would be working.

Making a mental note of what he was saying, I said, "Okay," and turned to continue my conversation with our visitors.

A few minutes later, Jerry was back in the kitchen with us, once again placing the aerial chart on the table in front of me.

"I want to make sure you know exactly where I'll be flying tomorrow," he said.

A chill ran across my heart, and I looked up at him and asked, "Why are you showing me this so many times? Do you feel like something is going to happen tomorrow?"

Shrugging his shoulders, he said, "I don't know. But if anything does happen, at least you'll know where to tell them to go looking for me."

★★★★

Usually when Jerry got up early in the morning to leave for a flight, he was up and gone before I realized what was happening. But this morning, he took more time than usual. Only half asleep by now, I could hear him heating water for coffee, and then I heard the hot water heater come on as he prepared to take a shower. Still in and out of sleep, it seemed to me that he was taking an unusually long time to leave that particular morning. It was almost as though he didn't really want to leave. Suddenly, I realized that he was back in the bedroom with me. Waking up completely, I called him over and put my arms around him. "Be careful," I said. I had told him to be careful so many times it had become a ritual for us when he was going on a flight.

"I will," he said as he put his arms around my pillow and lifted my head to kiss me good-bye. A few minutes later, I heard the whine of the car motor as he pulled away from the house and left for the airport.

Durango is in a plains-valley at the edge of the western flank of the Sierra Madre mountains. At 6,250 feet above sea level, the air is light and free of pollution and haze. Except for the summer months when it rains every day, Durango can boast of nearly perfect flying weather year round.

That morning, Jerry was giving a flying lesson to a missionary colleague before leaving for his trip south. Dub Williams had been in Mexico for a few months and had decided he wanted to learn to fly.

> The runway was rising alarmingly fast toward the Cessna 170B's main gear wheels. Since I was supposed to be doing the flying, it was my responsibility to halt the impending crash. My instructor, Jerry Witt, was emphatically reminding me that I needed to pull back on the controls if I intended to avoid disaster. In the nick of time, I did so, but probably not soon enough. My effort was rewarded with a reasonably smooth landing and the return of Jerry's perpetual smile to his face.
>
> Jerry was more than my flying instructor. Although we were both only 21, he was also my senior missionary. He had been on the field for over a year; I had only 4 months' experience. He grew up in a missionary home learning the Spanish language and culture, while I was still in chapter 6 of my grammar book.
>
> This particular morning was another example of his advanced status. He had several hundred hours of flying time, while mine could be measured in minutes. This was my first lesson, and Jerry was my first instructor. [5]

After finishing the flying lesson, Jerry and Nicolas took off for points south, over into the neighboring state of Zacatecas. As they gained altitude, they could see the beautiful Sierra Madre all around them. To the west, there were peaks jutting 14,000 and 16,000 feet into the air. To the north, there were a few ranges before hitting the big "laguna" area and the desert. To the south, there were more mountains, and it was into these mountains they were going to fly that morning.

During this year of our Lord, 1964, Mexico still had innumerable small towns that had little or no communication with the outside world. Most of them had no telephone, radio, television or even a reliable road system. Desiring to take the Gospel into even these remote areas, several pilots became involved in what was called "dropping" or "bombing" these towns with the Gospel of St. John. Flying only five hundred to six hundred feet above the terrain, they dropped copies of the Gospel of St. John into these villages. The Gospels had a form to fill out if a person wanted more information or if they wanted to order a correspondence course on the Life of Christ. These pilots never used anything written by man—no tracts or pamphlets. Their feeling was that the Word of God has God's promise on it not to return void, so it was only for the Word of God that they would risk their lives to take into these remote areas.

It was dangerous work, not only because of the low-level flying, but because of the persecution of evangelicals during that time. There were times when people on the ground threw rocks up at the airplane, occasionally hitting it. One pilot looked down at the ground as he passed over the village and saw a man pointing a rifle at him. Jerry was constantly receiving threats about his flying. Just a few days before his death, a lady came in from a village up in the mountains to bring a warning that had been passed on to her.

The warning was: "You tell that American pilot friend of yours that if he ever flies over this village again, we will shoot him down."

It was into that area that Jerry headed that fateful morning of April 8, 1964.

Flying due south for some 100 miles, they passed over the territory still belonging to the Tepehuan Indians, on into the state of Zacatecas, soon arriving at the north-south oblong valley that Jerry showed me on his aerial chart the night before. It was here that he and Nicolas were planning to drop 3,000 Gospels of St. John into the isolated villages. Working systematically and steadily, they covered the entire valley in a couple of hours and were looking forward to stopping off in the mountain village of Los Charcos for an afternoon service before heading to Durango.

Trini was an eight-year-old girl in one of those villages, and as the blue and white airplane zoomed back and forth across her town, she and the other children were running up and down the dirt streets, shouting and yelling at the airplane while the adults came out of their houses to see what was going on.

"Hey, you, kid!" shouted one of the men. "Bring me that thing you picked up from the plane."

Knowing that there were others he could get later, the child obeyed. By the time the airplane droned off into the distance, most of the adults knew exactly what the propaganda was that the airplane had been dropping. Within a few minutes, the village religious leader was in the central plaza demanding that everyone bring the Gospels of St. John to him.

As they slowly obeyed him, he put all the Gospels of St. John into a pile at his feet. Feeling certain that he had all the Gospels that had been dropped, he suddenly struck a match and made a bonfire of God's Word that had rained down from heaven that morning.

Trini's aunt, however, refused to obey. She didn't make a scene about it, she just calmly took the copies of St. John that Trini and some of the other children brought her and hid them under her mattress. No one but the family knew.

"That man has no right telling me what I can or cannot read," she muttered under her breath. "Especially since it is the Word of God."

For a long time after the rest of the town had forgotten about the day the blue and white plane flew over their village, Trini's aunt was still reading and pondering the things she found in her Gospel of St. John.

As Jerry and Nicolas pulled up out of the valley where they had been dropping the Gospels, Jerry suddenly spotted a good-sized town in the northern tip of the valley.

"We still have a few Gospels," he shouted to Nicolas. "Let's finish them up on that town below, okay?"

Smiling, Nicolas nodded in agreement. Zealous for the Gospel, he was willing to do whatever was necessary to get the Word of God to His people.

So, banking the plane into a turn, pulling on its flaps, slowing the speed of the airplane down and loosing altitude, Jerry and Nicolas came in over the town of Las Minas Coloradas, Zacatecas, to leave with them a portion of God's Word.

It was a bigger place than they had expected, and it took several passes to cover the entire town. On the first two or three passes, everything was normal. The people were running out into the streets, picking up the Gospels with the children running everywhere, wild with excitement. But on the fourth pass, there was a sudden loud noise, and smoke began to boil out from under the engine cowling and into the cabin. Abandoning the dropping of the Gospels on the village, Jerry banked the plane around in the opposite direction, turned off the ignition to stop all gasoline flowing into the engine, pulled on the flaps even more to slow the plane down and headed for a small road he saw on the other side of the canyon.

Whether Jerry was wounded and/or lost consciousness we don't know, but just as he reached the other side of the canyon, the plane suddenly did a nose dive and crashed into the canyon. The altitude was eight thousand feet above sea level. The estimated speed of impact was 140 miles per hour. The engine and nose section on the plane were buried in the ground all the way to the dashboard. The airplane exploded into a huge fireball that threw the right wing down the side of the mountain and destroyed everything except the tail section of the airplane. Jerry and Nicolas were in the presence of God.

About ten minutes later, three "campesinos" (country folk) came along on the same road Jerry had been trying to reach. They were taking a load of cactus apples into town to sell. Although they saw the plane crash, they knew nothing about what it had been doing in those parts. The wreckage was still burning, so the men threw dirt on the flames to put out the fire.

Then one of them walked into the town that Jerry had been dropping with the Gospel of St. John to let them know about the crash.[6] Since it was a mining village, it did have telegraph service, and they sent a telegram to Torreon, who, in turn, sent a telegram to Durango to let them know the plane crashed and that it had to be investigated.

Sometime during the day, these people loaded Jerry's and Nicolas' bodies, into the back of a pickup truck and took them to Sombrerete, Zacatecas, which was the county seat for that area and where all the legal work had to be done for the burial and transferal of the bodies. Because of the tremendous religious animosity and fanaticism, the bodies of these two evangelicals who had dared to "invade" their territory were strapped into two chairs and put on public display in the town plaza. During the afternoon, hundreds of people came by to see what had happened to these "invasadores."[7] They spit on the bodies, laughed, called them names and generally made fun of the two men who died bringing the Gospel to that part of their state. Some time later, the bodies were taken to the cemetery for burial.[8]

****

For the boys and I back in Durango, it had been a normal day. I had a Spanish lesson that morning, and as I was driving back home and passed the Plaza de Armas in downtown Durango, a band of intense pain gripped my head. Within a few seconds, it was released. This happened around 11:30 a.m.—the time of the accident.

When Jerry return from a flight, he always flew over the house to let me know that I should go out to the airport and pick him up (no telephones, you know). By late that afternoon, I realized I had not heard the sound of Jerry's plane flying over and decided to bundle up the boys and drive out to the airport to see if possibly I had missed the signal. During that trip out to the airport, I noticed there was a strong wind. When I got to the airport, they said he had not come in yet.

It occurred to me later that they probably already had the telegram concerning the crash even when I asked if he was in, but they didn't want to tell me.

It's hard to explain, but I didn't really expect Jerry in that night. I thought he might have had engine trouble, gone through a forced landing or something like that. Never in my wildest dreams did I suspect the truth.

It was only a few minutes after I returned to the house from my trip out to the airport that our doorbell rang. As I opened the door, I found a pilot friend of Jerry's standing there. Coming into the house, he closed the door and told me to sit down. As I sat on the sofa, he spent several minutes just walking the floor, pacing back and forth in front of me.

Finally, he turned to me and asked, "Where's Jerry?"

Feeling a little suspicious of his question and thinking it was really not his business, I answered, "He left early this morning for Los Charcos."

"You haven't heard from him at all since he left this morning?" he asked as he continued to pace back and forth.

"No," I answered, still wondering why he should be asking these curious questions.

"Are you sure he's not back yet?" he asked, still walking back and forth across the floor.

"Yes, " I said, "I am sure. I just came from the airport, and he still hasn't come in."

Even as he continued to walk back and forth, and it was obvious that he was distressed, not one germ of suspicion of the truth entered my mind. He finally stopped pacing and came and stood in front of me.

"It looks like Jerry was killed this morning," he said as he looked down at me. "We think his plane crashed in the mountains of northern Zacatecas."

Staring back at him, I did not believe him. Suddenly, an idea came to mind.

"Are you kidding me?" I asked.

Clearly taken aback by such a reaction, the friend rubbed his hand across the hair and said, "Lady, I wouldn't kid about something like that."

"Well, why do you think it was Jerry that was killed?" I asked, still not believing.

"I was at the airport when the telegram came in about the crash," he said. "I recognized the registration number of the airplane, and when I checked the number against the list of planes that had signed out from the airport this morning, the numbers matched, and Jerry's name was beside the number."

By now he had finally sat down on the other couch. With the truth trying to seep into my own spirit, he continued to talk about the different details that had led up to his realization that the destroyed plane was indeed Jerry's.

"The wire says that the wreckage burned and the only part of the plane left intact was the tail section, which has the registration number on it. The wire also said there were two bodies. One American and one Mexican."

"Yes," I said. "Nicolas was with him."

"Nicolas who?" he asked.

"Nicolas Cazares," I answered. "He was a friend of ours, and he was with Jerry in the plane."

We just sat there. What should I do? I didn't know. The pilot friend didn't know what to tell me to do, either. I still didn't believe it. I had three little boys alone with me in that house, and I couldn't walk out to go make telephone calls or look for people to help me in this situation. Just for a few minutes, I was in a complete stupor, and I needed someone to tell me what to do.

It was about this time that Dub and Deloris Williams walked in. He was the friend who had taken the flying lesson with Jerry that morning. The officials at the airport had been looking for him also, and he had come by the house to see if I knew what was going on. He took one look at my face and knew it was far more serious than he had dreamed. Not one word was spoken, but as he walked in, he sat down on the couch beside me and began to whisper, "Jesus, Jesus, Jesus!"

Leaving his wife, Deloris, with my children, he drove me down to the hotel where we always went to make our telephone calls. The only people I could think to call were my parents in Georgia. As Dub and I rode along to the hotel, I said, "Dub, I just don't believe it. I just do not believe that Jerry is dead."

Cautiously, he answered, "Well, it would certainly be wonderful if it turned out not to be true."

Even as I talked to my dad on the telephone, I said, "They say that Jerry has been killed." In the back of my mind was the thought that in the years to come, Jerry and I would laugh about the day everyone thought he had been killed.

When I got through to my parents' home, the only person there was my fifteen-year-old brother, Butch. Everyone else was at the church. I had forgotten that it was mid-week service night. The church didn't have a telephone, so I told Butch to go get Daddy and have him back at the house in fifteen minutes. I would call back.

Butch ran the entire mile to the church and interrupted the service to get Daddy to come to the telephone. As he left the service to drive to the house, my dad stood up before the congregation and said: "I have an emergency telephone call from Nola. I am afraid it is some kind of bad news about Jerry. People, please be praying."

A few minutes later, he was back at the church saying, "It is indeed bad news. Jerry has been killed. I am leaving for Durango as soon as possible to help Nola and the children."

Up until this time, I had been in such a stupor that I couldn't reason. I didn't believe that Jerry had been killed. It wasn't until after I talked to my dad on the telephone and he had believed what the airport officials were saying that it began to be true to me also. It was there in that telephone booth, in that hotel lobby after hanging up from talking with my dad, that I broke down and cried for the first time. Still, I felt this enormous need to keep my emotions under control. I didn't want people to see me crying and feel sorry for me. So before I went back out into the lobby and left with Dub to go back to my house, I made myself stop crying, dried my eyes and tried to face the world.

Still, how could such a thing be true? Didn't we love God? Yes. Weren't we serving God as He had commanded us by taking the Gospel into the whole world? Yes. Hadn't God promised to be with us always? Yes. So how was it possible for someone who loved God, who was obedient to His command, and who was doing everything He could to serve God in every possible way to die at such a young age with so much to give? How could a loving God take him away from his wife and three little boys? Boys who needed their father. Little boys who were only four years, two years and seven months old. How could such a thing be true? I didn't know. It made no sense to me.

The only telephone call I made about the crash, either in Mexico or the United States, was that one call to my dad, but somehow the word began to spread like wildfire. One group of friends was at the Polish Ballet, which was performing in Durango that night, and just as the first curtain was going up, someone whispered to them, "Did you hear about Jerry Witt?"

"No," they answered. "What happened to Jerry."

The reply came, "He was killed this morning in his airplane."

These friends, a man and his wife, could hardly sit still until the first intermission so they could get to our house and see about the children and myself.

In a couple of hours, the house was filled with friends who came to help in any way possible. Three of our friends, Max, Dub and Dan, left that night in Dub's pickup truck for the crash area to see what could be done about getting the bodies back to Durango for burial. Because Max was a miner, he knew where Las Minas Coloradas was located and was able to take the group directly to the site of the crash.

Just before they left, Max took me off to one side and asked if I had any special requests or instructions concerning Jerry's body.

"Yes," I said. "The only thing I want is for you to be certain that it really is Jerry. And if it is, please bring me back his wedding ring. It has his initials and the date of our wedding engraved inside."

The three men drove several hours that night and finally located the exact spot of the crash way up into the mountains of north Zacatecas. They were led to the spot by the fire of the watchman who were left to guard the wreckage. They got out of the pickup truck. Their flashlight beams pierced the night down to a place about fifteen feet below the road on which they were standing. The wreckage was still smoldering. One of the wings was leaning against a pine tree, and except for that and the tail section, the plane had been destroyed in the explosion. The ignition key was in the "off" position.[9] The identification number was intact, and any idea they may have entertained about it not being Jerry who had crashed was dispelled when they saw that number. It was Jerry's plane all right. And it was obvious that both he and Nicolas had been killed.

The watchman told them that the bodies had been taken back to Sombrerete.

Turning around and coming back down the mountain along the same road they had just come up, Max, Dub and Dan wound up in the little town of Sombrerete around 2 a.m. They checked into a hotel on the main plaza and tried to get some rest.

But they weren't able to sleep. One after another, they told stories about things Jerry had said and done, some of them humorous.

Dan said, "The last time I saw Jerry was just a few days ago when the male quartet for the English Sunday school was practicing. They were singing a song called 'My Father Planned It All.' After we finished practicing, as Jerry was leaving the auditorium, he turned around, raised his hand and said, 'Just remember Richard and Dan. Whatever happens, my Father planned it all.' "

Dub told about the time he and Jerry had been dropping the Gospels of St. John on a village when suddenly they hit a stretch of really bad downdrafts. Ordinarily these downdrafts present no danger, but when a plane is only five hundred to six hundred feet off the ground, they can be threatening.

"You can imagine what I was thinking," Dub said. "It was one of my first times in a small plane like that, probably my first dropping trip, and there we were in these terrible downdrafts. As Jerry literally wrestled with the airplane to keep it under control, I was tense. Because of this anxiety, I was squirming a bit, and inadvertently my shoulder hit the latch that was holding the window in place. Suddenly, not only were we wrestling with downdrafts, but a strong wind blew into the airplane. I thought we were goners.

Because of the heaviness of their hearts, they had not been able to sleep much that night, so they were waiting for the officials when the offices opened the next morning. They already had been out to the cemetery to positively identify the bodies and were now back at the offices to take care of whatever needed to be done. The receptionist told the mayor that these men were there about the American's crash the day before, but the man ignored them.

Dub was restless, but Dan and Max counseled patience, and after more than two hours of waiting, the mayor finally decided that he could see the Americans and find out what they wanted. Sombrerete was one of the towns that had been dropped with the Gospels of St. John the day before, so everyone knew exactly who this "gringo" was who lay dead out at the cemetery. There was no sympathy or even cooperation on the part of the officials. The men went back and forth between different offices all day long. And every place they went they had to pay more money. Dan said that he cannot even begin to estimate the amount of money they paid out in bribes to get all the necessary papers and signatures, but it was a lot.

At 2 p.m., everything closed down tight, and any papers they still lacked had to wait until 4 p.m., when everything opened again. During this time, the three men went out to the cemetery again. Max began to look for Jerry's wedding ring. Not finding it on the body, he began to inquire around and discovered that the mayor had the ring and was waiting for someone to offer him money for its return.

Max was furious. He told the man, "You can either give me the ring voluntarily, or I will take it away from you."

He didn't want to have to pay a bribe to get the ring back, but that is what they eventually wound up doing, just as they had to pay a bribe for everything that was done that day.

The scene at the cemetery was not nice. The bodies had been placed into rough wooden boxes and were on public display. There had been no attempt on the part of the authorities in Sombrerete to notify anyone. The mayor had ordered that the men be buried together in a common grave with no funeral honors. There would be no consideration given, not even the services of one of the several religious leaders who were present. By the time our friends arrived on the scene, there were approximately two thousand people who moved like a huge river toward, in and around the cemetery.[10] Word had spread that the evangelicals who had dropped the Gospels of St. John from the airplane the day before were now lying dead at the cemetery. There were so many people lined up to see the bodies in their open wooden boxes that even the traffic on the main highway was disrupted. The men who had gone to bring the bodies back, saw the remains of their friends displayed before the gawking eyes of the amused mob. Fighting tears and feelings of anger, the men were hurt still more by the mirth that was expressed by those people who walked by to view the charred bodies of their friends.[11]

Besides those in line to view the bodies, hundreds of other people were milling around in a carnival atmosphere of rejoicing. The parochial schools had been dismissed, so there were dozens of children around. Sound trucks were playing music. Ice cream trucks were selling their products. Tacos were being sold from stands. People made no secret of their elation over what had happened to these two men.

But, after still more trips to offices and dealing with uncooperative officials, Dub, Max and Dan were finally able to load their friends' bodies into the back of the pickup truck and leave for Durango.

4

In the Meantime....

A s soon as my father hung up the telephone after talking to me, he began to make arrangements to leave for Mexico. There were no flights from where he lived into Durango at that time, so he called a friend in San Antonio.. David Coote was the president of International Bible College, and he agreed to meet my dad at the airport in San Antonio. As soon as my dad arrived, they planned to leave immediately and drive the remaining 750 miles to Durango in Mr. Coote's car. Still, they were uneasy about making such a long trip so late at night without someone along who knew the language and the country. As Mr. Coote pondered these things in his heart, he walked around the corner of the boy's dormitory on the IBC campus and practically collided with Martin Fessler, a missionary from Monterrey, Mexico. Martin agreed to make the trip with them.

★★★★★

All that night after the men left for Sombrerete, Zacatecas, those of us in Durango waited. The next morning, we waited. The next afternoon, we waited. On into the night, we all waited for that pickup truck with its precious remains to arrive back in Durango.

During the day, people were coming in and out of the house and offering their help in any way we might need it. The government inspector from the airport came and brought his aerial charts with him. It seemed he was confused about the exact location of the crash. There were two towns in the state of Zacatecas with the same name.

But because Jerry had insisted on showing me the exact spot where he would be flying, I was able to point it out to the inspector. It saved valuable time.

Someone else took care of my children and made certain they were fed, bathed and put down for their naps. I was still in a stupor, not really understanding a lot of what was happening.

One thing I did understand was that the men in Sombrerete were taking an awfully long time to get finished with the paperwork and get back to Durango. At around noon, Max called his wife to say he thought they would be finished at around 2 p.m.

At 2 p.m., the telephone rang.

"All the offices have closed up on us," Max said, "and it looks like we're going to be here a while yet."

In the meantime, other friends of ours were trying to make arrangements for a brief funeral service in Durango before we left for the burial in San Antonio. But how could we make plans for a funeral service when we couldn't get a secure word about when they would be back into Durango with the bodies?

Around 4 p.m., Max called again.

"It looks like they're going to make us wait still a little longer," he said. "We haven't been able to leave yet."

At 6 p.m., the last telephone call came.

"We're leaving. We should be there in about three hours," he said.

Other telephone calls came in during the day as well, including one at around noon.

"We're in Monterrey and should be there around nightfall," Martin said.

However, at around 4 p.m., they called again from Torreon.

"We've had some bad traffic, so we're not going to be in until around 10 p.m."

That also became the decided upon time for the funeral. Both the group from Sombrerete and the group from San Antonio should be in by then.

Long before 10 p.m., a group of people already had begun to

gather at the auditorium of the Colegio McDonell in Durango, where the service was to be held. Some of the Mexican church members had been waiting all day with us for some word from the group of Sombrerete.

A little before 10 p.m., word came to me at my home that the men from Sombrerete were back and that the bodies were being turned over to the funeral home in preparation for the services at the school. Two of my friends had gone to the funeral home earlier that day and picked out both the coffins. When it came time to go to the service, someone came and picked me up. Someone else made arrangements for baby-sitters for my children. I don't remember who did either of those things.

The group from San Antonio still had not arrived, but it was decided to begin the service anyway and leave someone out at the crossroads waiting for them to lead the way to the auditorium where the funeral was being held.

About twenty minutes into the service, Martin Fessler walked into the auditorium, followed by David Coote. Behind them, hesitating in the vestibule and looking for me, was my dad. The group from San Antonio had arrived. As I ran into my dad's arms, I cried for the second time—but not much. I still didn't feel I could really turn loose and cry the way I felt, or I would lose complete control and somehow fail Jerry during this important time of our marriage.

Early the next morning, Max was at my home with the wedding ring that I had asked him to bring back to me. Max owned a rock shop, and he had taken the ring, polished it and cleaned it up from the effects of the fire, and it looked like new when he gave it to me. Here was more evidence that Jerry was gone. Slowly but surely, the truth was seeping into my soul.

Thanking Max for all his help, I took the ring and went back into my bedroom. That still wasn't far enough away from the ears of all those who were in the house, so I went into our closet and closed the door there also. Holding onto his ring tightly in one hand and the sleeve of one of his sport coats in the other, I buried my face in the folds of the jacket and began to let some of the grief come out.

Feeling as though I were talking to Jerry, I cried, "Oh, Jerry! How can such a thing have happened? How will I live without you? I'll never marry again!"

Almost as though Jerry were listening to me, in my mind I heard his voice say, "Oh, yes you will. I want you to marry again. My sons need a father, and you need a husband, so don't go making promises that are not yours to keep."

Even in the closet, though, I still was not able to escape the responsibilities of the day. Suddenly someone was knocking on my bedroom door and calling "Nola. Nola. Are you all right?" Wiping my tears again and straightening my face, I came out of my bedroom and made another effort to deal with the world.

This day was another entire day that consisted of waiting. During that day, more people continued to offer their help. Suddenly, a childhood friend of mine married to a Mexican pastor was in the room with me. I didn't even know she was there until she put her arms around me and asked, "Nola, is there anything we can do to help?" She and her husband flew up from Tepic, some four hundred miles south. When they saw that everyone was waiting, they decided to wait also.

Her husband, Joel, was perfect for handling the telephone calls and inquiries from the radio stations and newspapers that wanted information about what had happened. At that time, there was still a good deal of persecution of evangelicals, and several of the people were afraid to say boldly what Jerry and Nicolas were doing for fear that it would cause trouble for other evangelical friends throughout the state. However, Joel had no such inhibitions, and he gave an interview to a reporter from our local newspaper who had been at the house a couple of times but with whom no one wanted to talk. Joel told the entire story, and the next day, the story on the front page of the paper was headlined "The Two Men Who Died in the Crash Were Evangelical Ministers." There was a picture of Jerry on the front page, with our family's picture on an inside page, as well as a picture of Nicolas and his family.

Sometime that day, my friend Carolyn Ross took me to the bank to take all of our money out of the account and to cash some other checks that had come. We needed everything we could get to make the trip to San Antonio. At the bank, another surprise awaited me. One of the officials told me I could not take the money out of our account. Even though it was a joint account, and my signature was valid, he had read in the newspaper that morning about Jerry's death and the entire account as well as anything else I might deposit even now would be frozen until such time as the government would decree that I was Jerry's legal heir and had a right to the funds in the account.

I didn't know what to do. I needed the money for the trip, and I needed the checks I held in my hand cashed. What could I do? As Carolyn tried to help me work through this, a friend of ours who worked at the bank learned of the problem and came to help. We gave him the checks, and he took them to the cashier's window and cashed them.

The reason everyone was still having to wait through yet another day was because even though the men who had gone to Sombrerete had battled long hours with officials there, they still didn't have all the necessary papers. They hadn't been able to get the death certificate from the doctor who performed the autopsy. So, instead of leaving the next morning for San Antonio for the main funeral and burial, someone had to go back to Sombrerete and get that one last paper.

A childhood friend of Jerry's, Chico Howard, volunteered to go. He didn't think he would be gone any later than noon because he left about daylight to be there when everything opened up. But again, it was an all-day ordeal just to get one paper signed by one doctor. Chico went straight to the doctor's office as soon as he arrived in Sombrerete, but he was told the doctor was not there.

"When will he be back?" he asked.

"In about thirty minutes."

"Well," Chico said, "I'll go get a bite of breakfast and be right back. Tell the doctor I've come about the death certificate on the American who was killed."

In thirty minutes, Chico returned. The doctor had returned and left again.

"Did he leave the death certificate?" he asked.

"No, sir. He made no comment when we told him you had come for the papers."

"Do you know where he was going?"

"Well, he said he was going over to the restaurant to get some breakfast."

Chico left the office and went over to the restaurant. The doctor was not there either.

Chico went back to the doctor's office and was told that again the doctor had been there but had left. And no, he did not leave the paper.

This went on all day.

Finally, Chico sat down on the front steps of the doctor's office and waited until he would eventually show up from one of his vaguely defined "trips" around town. He sat there for several hours but was rewarded when the doctor finally returned.

But the papers were not filled out. So Chico waited another two hours. The doctor said he was busy getting the information together for the paper. Altogether, it took 16 hours for Chico to get one death certificate for an autopsy that had already taken place the day before.

He got back into Durango after sunset and our little caravan, which consisted of the hearse, my car and Mr. Coote's car, was finally able to leave Durango and begin its pilgrimage to San Antonio. In the beginning, there were two coffins in the hearse. We stopped in Torreon and left Nicolas' body there with his family.

*****

Daniel Gutierrez was one of those friends who had been in and around the house since the word of Jerry's death. He'd made the trip to Sombrerete for one last look at his friend. Daniel had spent innumerable hours with Jerry as they had traveled from town to town and village to village looking for open doors through which they could pass to preach the Gospel. They had opened some ten missions in different places, and Daniel was the only person who knew where all these places were and the people involved in them. Just before we left for San Antonio, I spoke with Daniel and asked him to take care of the missions and see that the services were held as usual until we could make a decision about what was to be done on a permanent basis.

Exhausted myself, I noticed that Daniel's face was white with his emotions near the surface. He was exhausted.

"I'm sorry to ask you to do all this, Daniel," I said. "But, I really don't know who else to turn to. You're the only person who knows where all these places are located and the people who are involved. You're the only one who can help me with this."

Solemnly he nodded his head and assured me he would be glad to take care of this until something else could be arranged. It meant his making ten trips to different little towns every week and holding services, apart from pastoring his own small church in the city of Durango.

As we finished our conversation, I turned in response to something someone was asking me, and it wasn't until a few minutes later that I noticed that Daniel had moved away from me over to a big window and was looking outside at some of the children playing on the patio. Without making a sound, or moving a muscle, Daniel was weeping with the tears flowing continuously down his cheeks.

★★★★★

The trip to San Antonio went smoothly. At one point, while we were crossing the desert that night, it was quiet and cool with the sound of the car's motor in the background. It was a scene that Jerry and I had lived through many times during our travels. For a second, as I sat in the front seat of the car with my sleeping baby on my lap, it was as though Jerry and I were together making another trip, and I was content. Suddenly, my heart twisted as I remembered that I wasn't with Jerry. Indeed, Jerry was gone. We would never make another trip such as this together.

We had to stop in Monterrey, where the American Consulate officials were waiting for us and were to give us another big sheaf of papers to get us across the border. At the Mexican/U.S.

border, the coffin was turned over to another funeral home. The hearse with its coffin inside cleared through customs faster than we, the living, did. On the American side, still another funeral home took charge and notified the people in San Antonio of who was going to pick up the coffin and who was going to handle the service there. We stayed with the coffin all the way to the U.S. side of the border, where the funeral home would hold the remains until the people in San Antonio could come down and pick them up. My dad and Mr. Coote wanted us to go on into San Antonio without waiting so the children and I could get some rest. After asking Martin if he would stay with the coffin and ride back in the hearse to San Antonio, I felt free to leave.

I was leaving Jerry in the hands of a trusted friend.

One scene I'll never forget. As the coffin containing Jerry's body was wheeled into the funeral home at the border, my four-year-old son, Jerry Jr., and I were standing in the driveway watching. I was holding his hand, but suddenly Jerry Jr., left me and went to stand a few feet in front of me, only a small distance from where his father's coffin was being moved into the funeral home. It was as though he were drawn by the coffin, yet he had no idea of what was really happening.

****

Although I had personally only made one telephone call, by the time we reached San Antonio, people had begun to gather in from all over the United States and Mexico for the funeral. From the time of Jerry's death until the time of his final funeral and burial, six days had passed. On the trip up from Mexico two of my children became ill with some type of virus. and my sisters and mother had to take care of my children.

During all this activity, people in San Antonio had been desperately searching for Jerry's parents and family. His mother and father were finally located down in Central America and immediately began their trip back to San Antonio. His brother, sister, grandparents and cousins as well as my family were all in San Antonio from all over the continent by the time of his funeral and burial.

David Coote spoke the following words at the funeral:

"There's one picture in my mind I'll never forget. Why God planned and arranged it is God's business, but I am satisfied that He arranged it. The first time I saw this coffin, it was not alone. There was another one right beside it, at the same elevation, in the same hall there in Durango at around 10:30 p.m. The people were there holding a farewell service. As I walked in, it hit me that there were two coffins. Naturally, I had been thinking of Jerry, but I suddenly realized that there was another equally dedicated. His name, Nicolas Cazares. He was saved, washed in the same blood, and filled with the same Spirit. He, like Jerry, knew what it could mean, but he laid his life on the line...and as their hearts united in one common, glorious cause—the spreading of the Gospel—so they had been together in life, together in death and together in that funeral hall. God inspired my heart to point that out to those people who were there with us for that service. This had been a brotherhood—a joining of hearts. Together. They had one common purpose. This joining of these two people's lives in life and in death is symbolic of the joining together there must be between the missionaries and people of all cultures to get the Gospel out to the entire world."

Except for those who have gone through a similar experience, people don't understand when I say that many of the things that happened and many of the things that were said to me were never seen or heard. For example, I learned later that at the burial, I had walked off and left a long line of people waiting to speak with me and console me. I didn't see any of them. I didn't even know the line was there.

Even though the truth was gradually seeping into my mind, I was still gripped with the thought that I had a job to do. That job was to get Jerry's body back to San Antonio and have the funeral and burial services conducted in as triumphantly a manner as possible. If I broke down emotionally, I felt I might not be able to regain control, and that would be the end of my participation.

Jerry's funeral would be lost to me, and I would have failed his memory.

So I held onto my emotions with a tight grip. Many people marveled at my composure, but it was not composure. I was completely numb. The sight of that coffin with its precious remains consumed me, and I had to do what I felt to be my duty toward it.

It was on into the evening by the time the burial was over and everyone began to gather back at the Coote's home on the IBC campus. Jerry's family was there, my family was there, and several close friends were there. They were visiting with one another, laughing and crying as they told one story after another of something Jerry had done.

Suddenly, I felt I was suffocating. I had to get out of there. Leaving the house, I began to walk across campus in the darkness. And the grief began to spill out. I cried out my hurt and confusion to God. Why? Why? Why? How could such a thing as this have happened to someone who loved God as much as Jerry did? Why? It made no sense.

Finding a stone wall that stretched across one section of the campus, I climbed up on it and continued to cry my heart out to God. As I sat on the wall weeping, my mother came looking for me.

"Mama, I just don't understand it," I said. "I'll never understand how such a thing could have happened."

"I know," she said. "I don't understand it, either, but we have to accept it as God's Will."

Still crying, I said, "I know. I refuse to entertain the thought that the enemy could have done such a thing to Jerry, so I have to accept it as God's Will, but I still don't understand it."

"Anyway," I continued, "I had to get out of that house. Although I know they loved Jerry and mean no lack of respect to his memory, I simply could not handle any more laughing and joking when we have just finished burying Jerry. Everybody seemed like they were having too much fun."

After talking to my mother for a few more minutes, I again dried my tears, straightened my face and went back to trying to cope with this new world and its responsibilities that had been forced upon me. I knew it would not be easy, but it had to be done.

5

Picking Up the Pieces

The children and I went to Georgia with my family immediately after the burial. But I was restless. I felt I needed to get back to Durango. And people kept asking me the question, "Are you going back?"

At first I didn't know. Once I heard my dad say that he wouldn't permit me to go back to Durango alone with those babies. My first reaction was one of relief. At least that decision had been taken care of for me.

But, as the days wore on, I kept asking myself the same question. I wanted to go back, but should I go back? Months before his death, Jerry and I had talked about what I should do in case he was killed. We talked about what would happen with the little congregations God was raising up and if I should return to Mexico in case something happened to him.

"Actually," Jerry said, "you're the only logical person who could keep everything moving if something did happen to me."

Although I remembered that conversation, I did not feel bound by it in any way. But I had to go back, at least temporarily, because we had our furniture and a good deal of unfinished business that needed to be taken care of. So, a week after Jerry's burial, I was making plans to go back to Durango. Subconsciously, I think I was searching for Jerry, waiting for a telephone call or a letter. I think I had the idea that in Durango, I might find him.

Going back to our house was difficult. Some friends had

already packed Jerry's clothes away, but his books, his Bible and his study notes were still laying around everywhere. Instead of finding Jerry as my subconscious had felt I would do, I actually felt the loss even greater when I got back to our house and he wasn't there. Not only was he not there, but his things were being moved out also.

The numbness was beginning to wear off. The feeling was coming back. I began to take a mild tranquilizer to sleep at night. My nerves were frayed. Should I stay in Durango, or should I pack up and go back home? I tossed and turned at night seeking an answer. And always I asked myself, "What would Jerry want me to do?"

I knew what he wanted me to do because he had told me. He wanted me to stay in Durango and continue the work. But how could I possibly go back to live in a foreign country with my three little boys and take on the responsibility of the work with all its situations and problems? My heart cried out, "Oh, God, what should I do?" I did not want this. I had never desired to be the one in charge. All I ever wanted was to help Jerry. The most natural thing for me to do would have been to leave Mexico, get a job and try to rebuild my life. But, I was feeling more and more that the Lord wanted me to remain in the wreckage of my life and rebuild on the same spot.

✶✶✶✶✶

I was crushed beneath a load, so gigantic and enormous that I could scarcely breathe. Losing Jerry within itself was overwhelming, but being expected to carry on the work and raise my three boys at the same time, alone, made me despair. My soul experienced the very depths of agony. Jerry was such a tremendous part of the work and of my life that I couldn't see how the Lord could expect me to live through it all without him. How could I do this thing that the Lord was asking of me? I didn't know. How could I live without Jerry? I didn't know that either. Every time I heard a plane fly over, it was Jerry. Every time I went out to one of the villages for a service, it was Jerry. Everything I touched, everything I saw, it was all Jerry. There were so many things he had planned, so many things he wanted to do that would never be done now. He was so young and had so much of the promise of God on his life. God, how could such a thing have happened? Yet he was gone. The Lord planned it that way, but that didn't keep me from loving him and missing him so badly that it was like an illness shut up inside my soul that wanted to kick open the doors of my heart and scream in agony. If Jerry himself could only have come and explained to me that "My Father Planned It All." But he couldn't. I didn't know which way to go, what to do, or what to say. In my despair, I turned to the Lord. He was the only One who could help.

*****

In all this confusion and nightmare, God's presence was real. Although God had been the author of this tremendous blow to my life, He dealt with me gently and lovingly. There was a strong knowledge of God's patience with me in spite of my tears and my questions.

So, my three boys and I went back to Durango to try to continue the work that had been begun by Jerry. In God's mercy, I could not look down the road and see the frustration, heartache and grief that still lay in my path. But God was with us.

We began to pick up the scattered pieces. It was still unreal, like the worst nightmare of my life, but at least I began to function again.

On the day before the crash, Jerry and I had made a trip into the mountains to one of the villages where a group of believers was organized for the purpose of laying out and beginning construction on their church building. All work had stopped when Jerry died, and now it was up to me to get that building project moving again and the church finished. I knew nothing about building, other than that the walls went up. I knew nothing about the price of materials or labor, or the cost of putting up a building such as this. I hardly knew what was going on. No doubt that particular building contractor made a mint off me on that job because I had no way of knowing how anything should be done. (That church had to be rebuilt a year later because the contractor had cheated me. During a strong wind storm, the roof had blown off the building, and the walls were so weak they shook when we put a ladder against them.) But I was learning.

Another project that had been left hanging with Jerry's death was the building of a Bible school on the property that he had already bought about ten miles outside the city of Durango. At the time of his death, men had been hired to clear the property and try to get it ready for the initial building. Again, my lack of experience was a big hindrance, but slowly I was learning.

I didn't know, for example, that it is against the law in Mexico to cut down trees without a special permit from the government. Trees are considered a natural resource in this country, belonging to the government, and we were supposed to get permission to cut down the trees on the property. God must have protected me in my ignorance because we cleared about fifteen acres of land with no permit of any kind. We were never reported for making this big mistake. Later, when we learned about the need for a permit, we secured one and cleared more land.

Friends and relatives came down and helped get the building project started. For a while, Jerry's dad, Dave Witt, was in Durango helping also. Then my father, Eugene Holder, spent two months running the work crew, pouring cement, and making and laying blocks. I also was involved during this time by being out at the building site, hauling dirt in the pickup that the workers would then use to make the blocks for the building. Sitting in that pickup (generally studying for a class) while the men loaded dirt into the back of the truck and then waiting again while they unloaded it at the work site, I often wondered how on earth I got into such a fix. Certainly, I had never sought such a job. It was something that had landed in my lap by default. But God gave the grace and strength to move through those weeks and months.

After my dad left, my sister and her husband, David and Rena Pitman, moved down to Durango on a permanent basis. David had the job of finishing up the first two buildings on the Bible school grounds.

Construction work in Mexico is different from the United States; David had numerous problems as he had to re-learn all the building trade and work with the limited supply of materials available in Mexico. There was one particular section of the roof that David could not get to work out right. No way he approached it was successful. For days, he lived with that problem trying to work it out until finally his oldest boy (five years old) prayed one day, "And Lord, help daddy to get out of the valley on that roof."

Slowly the buildings were built, and it was in January 1966 when we moved the Bible school operation out to the grounds. We already had begun the classes the year before but had rented some buildings in the city. Now we were on our own property.

Apart from the problems and responsibilities of the building programs, there was the responsibility for services in eight villages, ranging in distance from sixty miles north to seventy miles south of where we lived. We had only two national pastors working with us at the time of the accident, and one of them was killed along with Jerry. We were left with one pastor, eight missions and myself. Obviously, we couldn't take care of all that work, so a good friend of ours who belonged to another church organization filled in and helped with the services in some of the villages.

Traveling some one thousand miles each week, I drove constantly taking care of these services. Many times on Sunday, I drove eight hours without rest, going from one village in the morning to another small town for the night service. There were times when I felt overwhelmed with the problems and responsibilities, but I would feel the presence of God speak to me in a whisper, "Persevere!"

When Jerry died, I spoke little Spanish. Most of the time, it went over my head and I hardly knew what was being discussed. Soon after Jerry's death, I took an intensified language course in Mexico City through the American Embassy. I also studied with a private teacher in Durango. But, most important, I believe the Lord anointed my mind and gave me a facility for speaking Spanish.

During that time when I was struggling with everything, we felt that we needed to get the Bible school classes started. I had to stand up in front of a class of young people and teach for thirty to forty minutes and answer their questions. Although I knew it had to be done, when it came time for my class, I was petrified. I was afraid they would make fun of my Spanish. (They did.) I was afraid they wouldn't understand what I was trying to say. (Many times they didn't.) I was afraid I would make myself look foolish. (I did.) But the students seemed to appreciate my effort and with me stumbling along the way and their helping occasionally, we made it. I felt like a great battle had been won the day my first class ended. This went on in that manner for about a week, but by the end of that first week, I was moving more easily in the language and had more confidence. I made many more mistakes after that, but they didn't bother me. I was trying, and the Lord was helping, and that was what was important.

As the classes continued and the work grew, I became more and more dependent on others to help with my children, my house and the mechanics of the work. When Jerry died, we had one Peugeot automobile. He was planning to sell it. I knew nothing about the upkeep of a vehicle. How many pounds of air were needed in the tires? How often should the oil be changed? When should the car be greased? As a result of that lack of knowledge, I didn't change the oil for almost a year.

At the end of that year, I took the Peugeot into the dealership to get some work done on it. It needed an overhaul. When I called the mechanic to see how much it was going to cost and how long it was going to take to do the work, he asked, "Mrs. Witt, how long has it been since you changed the oil in this car?"

In my uninformed naivete, I replied, "It's been over a year. I haven't changed it since my husband's death."

"Why not?" he asked.

"Well," I reasoned, "I figured it was using so much oil anyway that it pretty much kept itself changed. I was having to put oil in every time I filled up with gasoline, and I thought that would be enough to change the oil."

But I was a fast learner. A good garage helped me learn some of the rudiments of maintenance, and after the overhaul, the

Peugeot gave another two years of good service.

Making trips to the United States for special projects and staying in touch with our supporters was also now my responsibility. In the fall after Jerry's death, I made my first trip of that type to Phoenix, Arizona. Leaving my boys with Baptist missionary friends, I flew in a DC-3 over the mountains of Mexico into Arizona. It was a successful trip all around. One thing I learned on that trip was that I was no longer afraid of flying. I had done a good deal of flying with Jerry, but I had done it with my emotions under tight control and only with the thought of sharing this experience with him. Also on this trip, I learned that I could speak before a large group of people for thirty minutes or more without becoming petrified or faltering. I learned that God was with me and that He was the One who would supply my every need in every area. It was a source of amazement to me that I would speak, and people would respond!

At this time in Mexico, it was necessary for U.S. citizens to make a trip to the border every six months to renew their personal papers as well as the papers on their vehicles. During the three-and-one-half years that I was alone as a widow, the boys and I never had to make this trip alone. God would always send someone to go with us.

One thing that was a constant source of surprise during this time was the way the Mexican pastors and brethren accepted me, a woman, as their leader. Mexico is a country that is famous for its "machismo,"[12] so for the people to accept me as a leader was a miracle. But accept me they did. God opened doors, anointed my teaching and worked with the people in a miraculous way.

Not long after the boys and I returned to Mexico, we were attending a picnic-type fellowship meeting with all the other missionaries in our area when one of the men sat down across from me at the table and said, "It looks like God is trying to speak through that situation in Sombrerete."

I was still numb enough to not really be able to capture what he was saying, so I just nodded my head in agreement.

A few weeks later, another friend made the same statement. This time I wasn't quite so numb, so I began to make some inquiries as to why they were saying that 'God was trying to speak through the happenings in Sombrerete.' I knew they were speaking about what had happened with Jerry's and Nicolas' bodies after their death, but I didn't really understand why they felt God was speaking through this situation.

At first, my friends were hesitant about telling me because they didn't really know how much I had heard about the happenings there. At that time, I didn't know there were rumors that Jerry had been shot down. I didn't know that their bodies had been placed on public display in the plaza. I didn't know about the problems the municipal mayor had caused with the legal work concerning the release of the bodies. I didn't know about the obstacles the coroner had placed in the path of the man trying to get the death certificate. I didn't know about the "discussion" Mr. Erwin had with the official to get Jerry's wedding ring returned. My friends had not told me that the parochial schools had been dismissed and that at least five hundred people were at the cemetery buying ice cream, selling tacos, playing music and generally rejoicing about what had happened to these two evangelicals who had dared to invade their territory. They didn't tell me that the people actually were having a party while Jerry's and Nicolas' bodies were on display out at the cemetery and our friends were in town struggling to get the necessary papers together to bring them back to Durango. All of these things were kept from me by my friends because they felt it would be too much for me to bear at that time.

But, reports of some things that were happening in Sombrerete began to come back to us, so they had to tell me these things to explain what was happening there.

There were two groups of leaders who participated in the situation on that spring morning in 1964. It was the religious leaders who had closed the schools so the children and teachers could go out to the cemetery. It was the religious leaders who had put the bodies on public display. However, it was the government or municipal leaders who had caused the problems with getting the necessary papers together. They were the ones who had caused our friends to sit for hours in his office waiting for his signature on different papers they needed. It was the municipal mayor who had caused these contretemps[13] and who had caused the wedding ring to be taken off Jerry's hand, holding it with the hope of getting some money from it. He was the one our friend had to deal with when he went looking for the ring.

Jerry was killed on Wednesday morning. It wasn't until Friday night that we finally had all the necessary papers and permits gathered together and were able to leave for the trip to San Antonio. Because of the distance that Jerry's parents had to travel and others who were coming in for the burial service, Jerry's funeral was held on Monday, and his burial was on Tuesday. However, on Saturday of that week, before we had even arrived in San Antonio, the main religious leader who had caused the disrespect toward the evangelicals' bodies was killed along with two of his fellow leaders when the pickup truck he was driving crashed on the highway near Sombrerete. They were all buried even before Jerry was buried. Two weeks later, the municipal mayor became ill in the morning, and they took him to Durango for medical treatment. That night, he was taken back in a coffin because he had died of a mysterious disease.

I don't tell these happenings with any sense of vengeance or anger. I simply relate them as something that happened during that spring and summer of the most tumultuous year of our lives. There was never any desire to get even with these people for what they had done to Jerry and Nicolas. Through it all, God's presence was so real it would have been impossible to try to do anything to take revenge for what had happened. Actually, because of these events, more missionaries were sent into this area, and, as a result, there are strong evangelical churches there today.

The information my friends had hoped to protect me from knowing became part of the process of coping and learning to trust God in everything.

Little by little, we were all adjusting, but the most traumatic adjusting had to be done by me and our three boys. So many people seem to think that because the boys were so small, they were unaffected by their father's death, but that is not true. The baby, Philip, was only seven months old at the time of the crash, and of all the boys, he showed the least immediate effect, but through the years, we've seen an insecurity in Philip that never appeared in the other children, and it goes back to losing his father at such a young age. He was always afraid for me to leave him. Whenever I would leave for a trip downtown or something like that, there was no problem, but when I would have to leave him with friends so I could make another of those trips for the work, he would go into hysterics. The events of that spring left him fearful, and he didn't really know why.

When Philip was about two, he became ill with tonsillitis. He couldn't eat and was running a high fever. A friend of the family was visiting us at that time, and I asked Joel to anoint Philip with oil and pray for him. He did, and as he finished praying, Philip looked up at him and asked, "Are you my daddy?"

"No, baby," Joel answered as he smoothed Philip's blond, curly hair back from his face. "Your Daddy is with Jesus."

Looking at Joel a few more seconds, Philip turned, laid his head on my shoulder and went to sleep.

The other two boys showed more visible reaction to Jerry's death. Mark was two years old and, again, most people didn't think he would be affected by what had happened. But just a few weeks after the crash, my mother found out that whenever Mark saw someone else crying, for whatever reason, he would burst into tears also. Even if it was something he would be watching on television, Mark would cry along with them. One day when this happened, my mother put her arms around Mark and lifted him onto her lap. She asked him, "Mark, what's wrong? What has happened?"

Lifting his little tear-stained face toward her, he pointed at someone else who was crying and he said, "Their daddy has gone to Jesus' house, too!"

When Jerry was killed, I had taken Little Jerry into a private room and explained to him as much as possible what had happened. I told him that his daddy was gone to live in Jesus' house now, and when a person goes to Jesus' house to live, they never come back here to live with us. Evidently, Little Jerry interpreted

"Jesus' house" to mean the church because the first time he went to church after the accident, he came to me saying that he had looked and looked for his daddy in Jesus' house, but he couldn't find him.

My dad felt that it was too much for Little Jerry to comprehend when I told him that his daddy would never be back, but while we were still in Georgia before returning to Mexico, something occurred that made him realize it was best for the child to know that his daddy would not be back.

One of my sisters had come by my folks' house to take me shopping. She, my mother and I left. My younger brothers and sisters were downstairs with my children watching television, so I didn't even tell the boys I was leaving. My dad was in the house with the children, and he said that a little while after we left, he heard a child scream, "No! No! No!"

Running upstairs he found Little Jerry sitting in the middle of the floor holding his head in his hands, rocking back and forth and crying hysterically.

"Jerry, Jerry. What's wrong?" he asked.

Still crying inconsolably, Little Jerry looked up at him and said, "My mommy's gone to Jesus' house, too."

Putting his arms around Little Jerry, my dad told him, "No, Jerry. Your mommy hasn't gone to Jesus' house. She just went shopping with Maw-maw and your aunt, and she'll be back in a few minutes."

Little Jerry believed my dad, and by the time I returned to the house, he had calmed down and was downstairs with all the children playing again.

Whenever Jerry was out of the city on a trip in his airplane, he always flew over the house when he came back to let us know that we should go pick him up at the airport. The boys were always excited when that happened and would go with me to the airport. For months after we were back in Mexico, Mark and Jerry still ran outside whenever a plane flew over our house. One time not long after our return to Mexico, Little Jerry and I were outside together when an airplane flew in low over the house. Looking up at the sky with his little four-year-old face glowing, he said, "Oh, Mommy! Our daddy's back after being gone for such a long time!"

The boys and I all missed Jerry and his airplane. There was an excitement about the airplane that was contagious and that stayed with us for a long time. Many years later, our own son, Little Jerry, was an adult man and had gotten his pilot's license and was flying his own airplane back to Durango for the first time. We were expecting him back that afternoon, and he was to "buzz" the house to let us know he was there. When he "buzzed" the house, there was a lot of excitement, and I jumped into our pickup and headed to the airport to pick him up. Suddenly, I realized it was the same excitement we had all experienced all those years before when Jerry would come in from a flight. It was an emotional time for me, and for the first time in more than thirty years, I wept for our loss.

For as long as a year after the crash, Little Jerry would talk about his daddy. When we had the dedication stone made for the Bible school, the stone was at our house for a few days before the dedication service, and Little Jerry would sit down in front of that stone and talk to it as though he were talking to his father. "Oh daddy," he would say. "I know you're at Jesus' house now, and I know you're never coming back, but I wish you could be here with me. I miss you so much!"

He was having the same battle I was having. It was taking time to emotionally understand that Jerry would never be back. More than a year after Jerry's death, one day as he sat at the table eating, Little Jerry suddenly said, "I wish my daddy would come back." Then shaking his head, he said sadly, "But, he won't."

My doctor told me about halfway through that first year that the work and my boys are what kept me going after Jerry's death. It gave me something to which I could dedicate my physical, emotional and spiritual energy. Something in which I was interested. Of course, I was overworked, but that work and my interest in it was what I needed. I was driving more than one thousand miles each week taking care of different services, teaching in the Bible school, supervising a couple of building projects and trying to be mommy to three little boys. There were times when I was so exhausted I hardly knew what was going on. On several occasions, I took a turn onto a one-way street going the wrong way, and even after I realized I was going the wrong way, it took me several seconds to realize where I was. My nerves were bad. I began to take tranquilizers again so I could sleep at night.

But, in all this, God was very real. During this time, I began to write songs for the first time in my life. One of them, "Unlimited,"[14] was based on the last sermon Jerry preached in English. I still did not understand why such a thing as Jerry's death had to be. But I accepted it as God's plan. My finite mind would never understand it all. There were many times when it seemed as though the Lord had turned His special care toward me. All during the time that we were alone, God always had someone with me in Durango helping with the children and encouraging me to keep going. One of those young ladies was Ruthie Fried, and one day after God had shown Himself so merciful yet again, Ruthie said, "God spends so much time taking care of you, I don't know how He has time to look after anyone else."

She was being funny, of course, but it was true that God did take care of us. My soul began to accept the fact that this work in Mexico was God's plan for me.

Having made a trip to Mexico City for some of my Spanish classes during this time, I had ridden the bus all night to get back to Durango. Now the sun was rising, and as we crested the hill some twenty miles out, we could see the city of Durango spread out in the early light on the plains before us. I remember that as I looked at that city spread before me, my heart rejoiced, and I said, "It is good to be back."

This was, without a doubt, where God wanted me. It was hard, but I was satisfied with the place that He had sent me.

6

"¡Así es la Vida!"[15]

Of course, my being satisfied that this was the place where God wanted me did not stop the problems and responsibilities from piling up. There had been several people who had volunteered to come down and help in the work, but seemingly nothing ever really worked out. One day as I was literally lying prostrate on the floor crying out to God about the need for help, the doorbell rang. My mother-in-law, Reba, was with us, and she answered the door. There stood a young man by the name of Lupe Hernandez, who had come from California to talk to me about the possibility of moving his family down to help with the work. It was a direct answer to prayer, even as I lay on my face.

Lupe and his family lived in Durango for about one year helping with the responsibilities. Other people came also, but most of them were there for only a few weeks or months at a time, until my sister and her husband, arrived and stayed several years.

Even with all the help, however, the final decisions and the final responsibility was mine. For example, one of the workers who had been with us for several months took our pickup truck into one of the mountain villages for a service one Sunday morning. Coming back to Durango, he had a flat tire. That night he was going to another town for the service, and he had another flat tire. That was two tires in one day. Taking the tires down to have them fixed the next day, I learned that they had been ruined. Both tires had been run while they were flat and the

87

repair man at the tire shop told me they were "like bubble gum inside." I didn't have the money to buy one tire, much less two, so the pickup sat out in front of my house until finances came in with which we could buy new tires.

Also, the tremendous financial responsibilities were mine. I had to distribute money for the needs of myself and my children, for feeding and housing the Bible school students, for the building projects, and for the support of the pastors and their families. Because we were under no board that guaranteed our support, we never knew from one month to the next what our income would be. Some churches made definite pledges, and we knew what we could expect from them all the time. But much of the support came from odds and ends, which meant that we never knew.

One-time finances were depleted, and although I ordinarily did not share any of this type of problem with the Mexican Christians, this time I had to go to the Bible school students and the Mexican brother who was helping and tell them there was no food and no money for food.

"It looks like we may have to suspend the classes," I told them.

They responded so positively that I came away encouraged.

The Mexican brother in charge of the students said, "We'll do whatever you need us to do. If you want, we'll go sell oranges, with chile powder, on the street corners and get enough money for food to keep us going."

"Yeah, Yeah, Yeah," shouted the students, more excited about the adventure than anything else.

"Well, just pray and hold steady," I said, "and we'll see what God will do."

The next day, money came in, and the classes continued.

Many times, we did not have food in the house. So we would go to the store to get our deposit back on the soda and milk bottles we had lying around. The supermarket let us take food in exchange for the deposit they owed us. Other times, we sold old, used tires to somebody who wanted to re-cap them so we could buy necessities. Sometimes we went for weeks at a time eating the bare minimum because income was low. Once, while my father was in Durango working on the buildings at the Bible school, we ate potato soup for several days at a time.

But we didn't complain. To some, it may seem demeaning that we had to sell bottles or tires to eat, but I was thankful that the bottles were there when they were needed. Even though we ate potato soup for several days, we had the soup. None of us really suffered. God was always faithful. Then, when it would seem that the absolute end was upon us, God always supplied. Time after time, God proved His sovereignty by supplying exactly what was needed at the moment it was needed. One of my professors in Bible College was always saying, "God is never in a hurry, but He is always on time." We found this to be true. Jesus never fails.

Most of the driving I did for the different services in the towns and villages was in a Chevrolet pickup truck. One Sunday, I began at 8:30 a.m. picking up people to take them to a baptismal service we had scheduled about thirty miles from the city of Durango. In Mexico, whenever it is possible, the Christians make a daylong affair out of a baptismal service. First, there is the service with those who desire baptism as well as the baptism itself. Then comes the time of eating and fellowship. Everyone brings his own lunch and shares it with his neighbor. Fires are built to heat pots of beans, and tortillas are heated on the hot coals. It is generally a time of good fellowship and sometimes games. Several churches go together and plan these services.

After driving for four-and-one-half hours, I finally rounded everyone up by 1 p.m., and we were able to begin the service. One of the Mexican pastors performed the baptisms, and this was always a time of rejoicing for the Mexican Christians. Baptism to them means that this is the final step, that final breaking with their old way of life. After the service, the lunch and the games, at 3:30 p.m., I began in reverse order to take everyone back to their homes. That Sunday, I drove that pickup truck three hundred miles, and the entire time, the radiator was leaking so badly that we had to stop and put water in it three or four times before arriving back at my house in Durango at around 8:30 p.m.

Actually, the day before that service, I had been driving the pick-up out to the Bible school grounds with a load of cement in the back when the radiator suddenly began to boil over and shoot steam into the air. This was before I learned a bit more about vehicles, so I didn't know what was happening. But some friends saw me on the side of the road and stopped to discover that the radiator was dry. The truck should have been put in the shop immediately to get fixed, but with that big baptismal service scheduled for the next day and all those people expecting and waiting for me, I asked the Lord to help me to hold off one more day, and He did. I went ahead and drove those three hundred miles that Sunday with the radiator leaking all the way.

However, that leaking radiator was the least of my worries with that truck coming back to Durango that day. The brake line was broken, and we lost all the brake fluid. I drove the last thirty miles of that trip with no brakes. How I got through the various intersections and traffic problems with no accident, only the Lord knows. By using the gear shift as my brakes, we made it home safely.

The next day, I took that truck to the garage, and we learned that the brake line had been smashed under the bed of the truck. We didn't suspect foul play, although the thought did cross my mind. After that trip, those brakes would go out from time to time, but we would repair them without really knowing what the problem was. One day while out at the Bible school property, again hauling dirt for the men to make more blocks, the brakes again began to get spongy, and one of the men looked underneath the truck and said the line was broken again and was loosing fluid. Time after time this happened, but we never did understand the problem.

One night, I was facing a trip back from a town some fifty miles south of Durango. It was late, and the brakes were gone. My children were at home with a baby-sitter, and if I didn't get back that night, the sitter would be frantic with worry. So after praying, I decided to head back. This was a fifty-mile trip on a Mexican national highway with lots of mountains and dangerous curves. Ordinarily, there was a lot of traffic on this highway (it was the main artery to Mexico City) with cattle strolling across the road at will. And to really make it interesting, we were making this trip at night.

Asking the Lord to clear the way before me, we left the little town and headed for Durango. Driving about twenty miles per hour, it took nearly three hours to drive that fifty miles, but we did not meet even one car or see even one cow or horse on the entire trip. That was a miracle. Not seeing the cattle was probably a bigger miracle than not meeting any traffic. When we came into the city of Durango, there was one main intersection where two main highways intersected that was particularly dangerous, but nothing was in sight. I drove that entire fifty miles from the church in the town fifty miles south of us, to the truck's parking place in front of my house without needing to stop once. Gearing the truck down with the four-speed transmission, we ground to a halt in front of the house—and praised God for His protection.

But we weren't through with those brakes yet.

Around this time, the senior class from International Bible College drove all the way to Durango to visit us and to work on their class trip. My brother, Buddy, was a member of this class, so he was their guide, and we had a great visit. They had been in Durango a couple of days, they had done some sightseeing, had visited some of the missions in several of the villages, and on their last Sunday morning, we were going to the mountain village to attend the church built soon after Jerry's death. We had to make the trip in the pickup because the bus in which they had come could not navigate the mountain roads (dirt) or ford the river to get into the village. So we all piled into the truck, eighteen of us altogether, and with my brother-in-law, David Pitman, driving, we left. The trip up was easy. There was only one case of motion sickness, even though the roads were curvy, rocky and dusty. We held the service, and afterward, we started the drive back out of the mountains to Durango. David asked me if I wanted to drive because he was getting tired, but somehow I didn't feel I should, so David was at the wheel again. That was the hand of God. David said later that he thought the brakes were getting spongy as he came through some of the mountain passes, but he wasn't sure and thought they would last long enough to get us all back home.

Sitting in the back of the pickup with the others, I knew we were arriving at the place where we had to turn off the main road bed and take a little trail down to where we forded the river. But David was not slowing down. Suddenly, we whirled off the roadbed onto the trail. The truck was moving fast, and I knew something was wrong. Everything happened so fast. Not being able to see what was happening ahead, I didn't know what was going on, except that David took another sudden turn and then we were all in the river—but not at the ford. David said later that as he approached the turnoff for the river, he tried the brakes, and they were gone. Knowing that the main roadbed led to a one-hundred-foot dropoff into the river, he realized that he had to get that truck down to the ford someway so the water would stop it. But, as he turned onto the little road that led down to the river's fording place, there was a huge wagon loaded with cabbage hitched up to four mules parked right in the middle of the road. Taking another quick turn, still heading for the river, the truck missed a huge oak tree by inches and ran down a grassy slope almost like a ramp prepared for us, right into the river. The truck was mired deep into the water and mud, standing on its nose, but it was stopped.

Those who had been riding in the cab of the truck saw it all, but those of us in the back only knew that we were in the river. As the truck stopped, the cabin immediately began to fill with water. David couldn't get the door open because we were in pretty deep water, but he rolled the window down and climbed out through it. One of the young ladies was so confused and panic-stricken that she didn't know which way she should go, and instead of walking behind the truck up the bank of the river down which we had come, she took off swimming across to the other side of the river.

"Hey, Lana," David shouted. "It's the other way!"

The class sponsors, who also had been riding in the cab with David, swam and waded around to the back to see if everyone was all right, and miracle of all miracles, everyone was fine. We all praised God right there. With eighteen people in the back of that truck and such a potentially fatal situation, only one broken thumb was reported out of the entire group. No cuts or knots or anything. Certainly God was faithful that day!

Even in the midst of this chaotic, muddy mess, there was humor. Seeing that everyone was all right, David and some of the other young men began to try to get the young ladies out of the truck and onto the river bank without their having to wade through waist-deep mud and water. They made chairs with their arms and everyone began to move out. All of the young men, except one, had gotten out on their own and were helping get everyone out and up on the banks. The man who remained in the truck had just bought an expensive pair of boots, and not only was he not going to get his boots wet helping take the girls out, but he stayed in the back of the truck until everyone else was gone and then told a couple of the guys that he wanted them to carry him out also. This guy was more than six feet tall, and he wanted to be carried out like the girls. The two guys he asked to help him were my brother, Buddy, and his roommate from college.

None of us on the bank knew what was happening, but Buddy and his roommate made a deal. Everyone was aggravated by that fellow, who expected someone to carry him when all the other guys had gotten out and were helping the others. Why didn't he just take his boots off? Buddy and his roommate picked this guy up in their "arm-chair," got him out into the middle of the river, shouted, "Now," pulled their arms apart and dumped him in the middle of the river. Everyone shouted and laughed. It was just another incident that made that afternoon one that none of us will forget.

The damage to the truck was considerable. The motor had to be dismantled and rebuilt, as well as other parts of the truck. But God had been faithful.

We never did discover what was making that brake line continually fail us. It could have been sabotage, but we never felt certain. But God protected us all the way.

The days continued to be full, hard and long. On some

Sundays, I drove from 8 a.m. until 10:30 p.m. On another trip into that same mountain village, we were driving along to the Sunday morning service. As we came around one of the curves, we suddenly met another truck on our side of the road, and he was going fast. Fortunately, he was also a good driver and swerved, managing to maintain control of his own truck and avoid what would have been a head-on collision. Still, he hit us and threw us into the side of the mountain, damaging the front of the truck. But again, God was with us.

In the three-and-one-half years I was in Mexico as a widow, in spite of the fact that I normally drove at least one thousand miles a week, I never had to change a flat tire. It seemed the tires always went flat when there was someone with me who could change it for me.[16] For that matter, in all those years of traveling alone or with the young lady who came and spent a year here with me, we never had any kind of mechanical trouble that left us stranded on the highway or even needing help. Mechanical trouble, we had. But it always occurred when the needed help was available.

Whether or not the brake lines were being sabotaged, we never knew. But of some things one can be certain. One Sunday night, I decided to attend a small church here in the city of Durango rather than drive to one of the villages because Philip was sick, and I didn't want to be gone so long. When we came out of the service, I found the rear window of my car smashed with rocks by the same boys who had been throwing rocks on the roof of the church during the service.

Another time, we drove to a village seventy miles north of Durango for its weekly service, and when we came outside afterward, we found that someone had punctured one of the tires. The tire was ruined. It had to be changed. This was at night in a village that had no electricity, so it was pitch black. Being well-prepared as always, I didn't even have a flashlight. When the men who were with me began to try to change the tire, the jack wouldn't work. They borrowed a jack from a neighbor and got the car jacked up. Then the lug wrench wouldn't work, and they couldn't take the lugs off the tire. The two brethren literally lay on the ground and laughed. Finally they got the tire changed.

No doubt we set a record for the longest tire change in history, but we could laugh.

However, some things brought us tears instead of laughter. An anthrax epidemic swept through the state of Durango the year after Jerry died, and among those who came down with the disease was a young Canadian nurse named Elizabeth Petkou. She was a missionary serving in one of the small towns in the state of Durango. She had trained for her nursing degree, had attended her missions' Bible school and then taken a year of language school. All this was done for the purpose of going to Mexico as a missionary. Less than a year after she had arrived on the field, Elizabeth came down with anthrax. Sick less than a week, she died only a few days after I had met her. Her desire was to be buried in the small village where she had served, but because of the nature of her death, health authorities would not allow her body to be transported over the county line. She was buried in the cemetery in the city of Durango before her family could get there for the funeral.

Another thing that we couldn't laugh about was the day one of the young men working on the buildings at the Bible school walked across one of the rafters to do some work on the roof and fell as the rafter broke. He fell about ten feet, landing on his head on the concrete floor below. He went into convulsions, writhing on the floor before lapsing into unconsciousness. David put him in the truck and headed to town, stopping at my house on the way to the hospital to let me know what had happened. By this time, the boy was beginning to regain consciousness but was out of his head.

As I drove my Peugeot behind the truck taking him to the hospital, I prayed: "Lord, don't let there by anything seriously wrong. Lord, don't let there be any brain damage. Lord, you see the situation. Heal this boy in Jesus' name."

And the Lord healed him. After spending a couple of days in the hospital with two doctors running numerous tests on him, the young man was given a clean bill of health. He even returned to continue working until the buildings at the Bible school were finished. God was faithful again.

The Bible school classes were in session by this stage of development, and one of the students who was with us during that first session of classes was an eighteen-year-old young man named Robert.[17] Robert was from a church fifty miles south of Durango, and despite opposition from his family, he came to study with us that term. We and the Mexican brethren were glad for a young man who had so much promise and who was determined to study the Word of God in spite of opposition.

After that term of classes, Robert got a job in a mine near Durango and would come by the house to visit us. On Sundays, he made the trip with us down to the village where his parents lived and where his home church was located. He made himself valuable to us in helping to keep the truck running, checking the tires and being around when something needed to be done.

Robert never did return to the Bible school, but he read books that we loaned him and seemed to be growing in the Lord. He decided to follow the Lord in the next step and was soon baptized in water. For a couple of years, he appeared to be faithfully serving the Lord.

Then, strange things began to happen. At first, we did not see any connection, but soon a definite pattern began to appear. We suspected him of being responsible for the problem with the brakes on the truck as described earlier in this chapter, but we were never certain enough to confront him about it. Then things like tools began to disappear from the truck. My car was broken into a couple of times, and the jack and lug wrench were stolen. Although Robert lived out of town and worked in a mine outside the city of Durango, every time something of this nature happened, he was around. Then my purse was stolen. Nothing valuable was lost, except my identification and driver's license. Since it happened in the middle of the week, I thought that certainly this time we could not suspect Robert because he would have been working; but no. Within a couple of hours after the purse theft, Robert showed up at the house. It turned out he was off from work because it was a national holiday.

My suspicions were being validated, and his attitude had changed so much that I was afraid to have him around the house any more. During one of his visits, he described to me how easy it would be to break into the house next door, which is where my sister and her family lived.

I said, "But who would want to break into their house? They don't have anything worth breaking into a house for."

"That's what everybody thinks," he said. "But the thief knows there are things that he could sell to make the robbery worthwhile."

One Sunday afternoon, he came around as usual, but this time, I didn't let him into the house. I felt certain he was at the root of all the pilfering. I stood at the door and spoke to him. As I stood looking at him, it was as though a spirit of evil permeated his whole being. All he could talk about was a man who had been killed up at the mine where he worked—the position of the knife, the way it had come out the man's back, the gory details of the condition of the body, etc. This made me more certain than ever that Robert needed to be watched. Some of the Mexican brethren hearing about the conversation in the Sunday night service insisted on coming home with me and spending the night because they knew he was in town and might show up at the house again.

The following Sunday, my three boys and I left as usual with a group of the brethren for the Sunday school services that were being held near Durango. Coming back to town, we went to a small restaurant, ate lunch and went back home. We were in the house for nearly an hour before I realized that something was wrong. The venetian blinds in my bedroom were hanging over the headboard of the bed instead of behind it. Some books I had left on the bed were rearranged and misplaced. As I began to look through the house, I knew that we had been robbed. Two of the bedrooms had been cleaned out. Binoculars, movie camera, sewing machine, slide projector, etc. Thousands of dollars worth of equipment had been taken. Among the things taken had been Jerry's wedding ring. Evidently, we had returned earlier than expected because they only cleaned out the two front bedrooms. Other things of equal value in the rest of the house had not been touched.

Immediately, I suspected Robert. I went next door to my sister's house where Daniel and Dolores Gutierrez were staying while my sister's family was in the United States and told them what had happened.

"You just wait," I said. "Within thirty minutes or an hour, Robert will show up."

When the other things had been taken, I had hesitated about going to the police because I didn't really want to cause trouble just in case I turned out to be wrong in my suspicions. But this time, I felt I had no choice. So I left Daniel and Dolores at my house with the boys while I went for the police, asking Daniel to keep Robert there if he showed up before I got back. Even as I pulled out of the driveway to go for the police, Robert walked up.

When I explained to the police everything that had been happening, they agreed that the problem with Robert was more than mere coincidence. Because he lived out of town and always showed up every time something was taken, he had to be involved. So, they went back to my house where he was still visiting with Daniel and put him under arrest.

Three days later, Robert's father showed up at my house asking where Robert was.

"He's in jail," I told him.

"Why?" his father asked.

"Because he has been involved in numerous thefts around here, and the police arrested him Sunday because of the robbery at my house."

He was calm and said he was going to the jail to see what was happening.

A few hours later, he was back at our house breathing "fire and brimstone."

"How dare you do this thing to my son?" he shouted at me. "I'll see that you pay for this and pay dearly. You and your children won't be safe any time you leave this house. You just wait and see. You're going to pay for this."

Pointing his arm and finger at one of my little boys standing at the door with me, he made the sound of a machine gun, "Rat-a-tat-tat!"

He continued to shout, using curse words, but I didn't recognize them because I didn't know any of those kinds of words in Spanish. I did well to learn the words I needed to know and hadn't acquired the ugly words. Incidentally, this man was supposed to be a Christian also.

A few minutes after he left, the sergeant in charge of the case came by the house to tell me that Robert's father had been to the jail and that he was angry. He came to warn me, but I told him that the man had already been to my house and some of the things he had said.

The sergeant was concerned enough about the threats that he put out a warrant for the arrest of Robert's father and put a twenty-four-hour guard on my house until he was found.

Word of what was happening went around through our missions and churches like wildfire. The pastor of the church fifty miles south of Durango sent his wife in immediately to stay with me when he learned of what was happening. Some of the other brethren and sisters were already with me. (A couple of them had spent the night on top of my house before the police put the guard on duty.) As Juana, the pastor's wife, got off the city bus and was hurrying toward the house, she was stopped by the police guard who was watching the house.

"Where are you going?" he asked her.

"I'm just going here to Sister Nola's house," she answered.

Looking at her for a few seconds, the police guard asked her, "What is she to you?"

Juana, not knowing that the police were guarding the house, shrugged her shoulders and said, "She's just my sister."

The guard didn't know what to make of that, but after looking at her for a few minutes, he told her to go ahead and go into the house.

Later when the sergeant brought his relief guard by so he could go off duty for a while, that guard was heard telling the detective: "I don't know what's going on around here. There have been people in and out of this house all day long, and everybody calls everybody else 'brother' or 'sister.' But they're not brothers. Some of them are Americans. Some of them are Mexicans."

The detective laughed and said, "Oh, that's all right. My sister married a Methodist, and all these evangelicals call each other 'brother' and 'sister.'"

That night, after the police picked up Robert's father, Robert's mother came to the house to see me. There she stood with a small infant in her arms, weeping and begging me to release her husband and son. Even as we were talking, the detective in charge came up to let me know that they'd picked up Robert's father.

"Sergeant," I asked, "what can we do in this situation? This is Ana,[18] Robert's mother, and she's begging me to drop the charges against both Robert and his father. What do you think?"

"Whatever you want to do is what we'll do," he answered. "However, the charges against Robert's father will not be so easily dropped because of the nature of the situation and because he also threatened some of the police officers in the jail. There is a certain procedure that will have to be followed in his case."

"Would it be possible to just drop the charges in my case against them, with the understanding that they will never come back around here again?" I asked.

"Yes," he said. "We can do that if you want."

"Would that solve your problem, Ana?" I asked the lady who was still standing there weeping.

Wiping her face with the baby's blanket she nodded her head, "Yes."

That night, they took the guard off the house because they had Robert's father in custody. Robert's father had to go before the state judge and pay a fine for having threatened my children and the police officers. Robert was held for a week and then released.

I never saw Robert or his father again. Although the thievery and problems with the vehicle stopped, it was still a defeat for all of us. These people needed the Gospel. They had known the Word of God for so many years, and still they had become involved in a situation such as that. It was hard to understand. It was my prayer that they found another church somewhere else and would be able to permit the Lord to really rule in their lives.[19]

Ruth Fried, who moved to Durango and lived with me for more than a year, helped with the children, the house, the office work, and, when I needed to be gone to raise money for the Bible school, she took care of the services in the villages. Using my vehicle, she drove one of the Mexican pastors to the different churches for their services.

On such occasion, Ruth and Maximilian (we called him Max) had driven into one of the mountain villages for Sunday school and were headed back to Durango. At least they thought they were. To get from this village to Durango, it is necessary to climb a rocky, winding, dusty road for about three miles before reaching the top of the mountain pass and before beginning the descent on the other side to the valley where Durango was located.

Driving my Peugeot, Ruth and Max started that three-mile climb. Suddenly, about halfway up, the car started throwing water and steam everywhere. The radiator was not holding its water. There they sat, halfway up the mountain, miles away from the nearest water supply. Certainly there was no water on top of that mountain. The only place they knew they could find water was back down the mountain, where there was a dry creek bed with a few puddles.

So they turned the Peugeot around and coasted back down to the valley out of which they had just climbed to those puddles of water. But when they got there, they discovered they had nothing with which to dip the water out of the puddle into the radiator. Frantically they searched the car for something to dip the water with, and came up with an empty Coca-Cola bottle. They filled the radiator with the water from the puddle and started back up the mountain.

This time, they made it a little farther, but still they didn't make it to the top. When they stopped the first time and the radiator boiled over, Max scalded his arm trying to take off the radiator cap. So this time when it started throwing steam, they didn't even raise the hood. They simply turned the car around again and coasted back down to the water. Again, they filled the radiator using the bottle. But again, they didn't quite make it to the top of the pass.

They had to turn around and refill that radiator using the bottle four times. The last time, they prayed over the car, got a good running start and made it to the top of the pass. But the radiator was steaming again by then, so they coasted down the other side of the mountain to water on the other side. They had to use that bottle a couple more times before they finally got back home, but they made it. They were thankful for that Coca-Cola bottle.

While Ruth was in Durango taking care of everything, I made a fifteen-thousand-mile trip on behalf of the work in Durango. Traveling from the West Coast to the Eastern Seaboard of the United States, I visited churches and pastors who had helped in the past and who continued to be interested in giving to the work in Durango. It was during this trip that I began to hear some of the rumors and criticism that were being leveled at me about my decision to return to Mexico and continue the work that Jerry had begun. The same message kept being parroted to me: "That's no job for a woman. A man needs to do it."

I agreed. The problems, the work, the heat, the traveling, the dealing with the pastors, trying to have a Bible school and, in general, the supervision of the work was certainly a job for a man. I agreed with them then, and I still agree with them. It was no job for a woman. I had inherited the work by default. Jerry was gone. What was I to do? Walk off and leave it all saying that it was no job for a woman? Deborah didn't shrink from going to battle, even though it was a job for a man. But, apart from my brother-in-law, David, no men tried to do anything about coming down and taking over. If a seasoned minister, one in whom I had confidence, had come down and said, "Nola, we feel like you need to take these babies and go home to your family. Don't worry about anything. We are going to take care of this work and see that these Mexican Christians are taken care of and nurtured in the things of the Lord. God has sent me to relieve you, and I will do it," then I would have left.

But no one ever did that. So I stayed in Mexico. My sister Rena and David were there. But even with their help, the work had grown to such a stage that we still could no longer handle all the responsibilities.

As I came back from that fifteen-thousand-mile trip, I was weary from the time spent on the road, and discouraged and disheartened about all the criticism I had encountered. I missed my children, and I missed my home. Somewhere in the sky between El Paso and San Antonio, wondering if it was all really worth it, I picked up the headset for the taped music that I found near my airplane seat. As I flipped on the switch for the music, it was as though the presence of God came and surrounded me. All that existed for me in those moments was the distant roar of the jets, the moonlight shining on the wing of the plane and the song being played in my ear:

> *When you walk through a storm, hold your head up high*
> *And don't be afraid of the dark*
> *At the end of the storm is a golden light*
> *And the sweet, silver song of a lark*
> *Walk on through the storm, Walk on through the night*
> *And you'll never walk alone*
> *Walk on, walk on, with hope in your heart*
> *And you'll never walk alone.*

God made those lyrics life to me. I was not alone, I had never been alone, and I would never be alone. He was with me.

7

Victory and Defeat

As with most churches or mission works, our story was one of enormous victories mixed with some bitter defeats. Although there was still a good deal of opposition in some areas in which we worked, in other towns and villages, the growth was steady, and new villages opened for the Gospel witness faster than we could take care of them. The Easter Convention, which had been inaugurated a couple of weeks before Jerry's death, became a yearly time of gathering all the churches and missions, and already the facilities in the newly built Bible school buildings could not contain all who attended. The year after Jerry's death, we began an annual Youth Camp. Since it was a new experience, and since neither conventions nor youth camps are run exactly as they are in the United States, there were many things to learn and unlearn. But, God was blessing and we were rejoicing at all the good things that were happening.

In the town fifty miles south of Durango where our only Mexican pastor was living at the time of the plane crash, we had a building rented in which the services were held. People began to gather from all sides and come to this larger town located in the midst of several villages. The room we had rented became crowded every Sunday night. We were accommodating more than one hundred people in a room that would ordinarily seat thirty to forty people.

That Christmas, we decided to show a movie about the life of

Christ in that little church, and there were so many people packed into that room that one could hardly breathe. Although I was operating the movie projector, I would have to leave the room through a side door near the projector so I could get some air. The place was so packed and the air was so stale that I felt like I was about to pass out. No one fainted, though, and no one left. They all stayed until the end of the movie. In that room on another occasion, the place was crowded by the time the service began. Suddenly, in the middle of the service, there was a crash and a shout. As we looked around, one of the overloaded benches had collapsed. There was plenty of excitement for a few minutes as everyone scrambled trying to find a new place to sit, thus overloading even more the remaining benches. But no one left. God was blessing, and crowded rooms and collapsing benches were nothing in comparison to the blessings of God. We were rejoicing! It wasn't long before we had bought property in that town and were laying the cornerstone for their church building.

Other villages were opening all over the state of Durango, as well as some down south in the state of Zacatecas and some up north in the state of Coahuila. We rejoiced especially about the contacts in the state of Zacatecas because they were a direct result of letters we got from people who had received the Gospels of St. John that Jerry and Nicolas had dropped from the plane the day of the crash. More national pastors came to work in the mission, and from the churches themselves came men who wanted to work in the Lord's vineyard.

The Bible school program also had proved to be a success. The original building was finished, and it was on the second anniversary of Jerry's death that the dedication stone was laid and the buildings and grounds dedicated to the work of the Lord. It had been a hard, tumultuous two years since Jerry had gone to be with the Lord, but God had proved Himself faithful time after time.

The Bible school students lived close to the missionary families. When discipline had to be meted out for numerous reasons, I had to stay right there with the students and supervise whatever they were doing. My boys were small, so I would take them along with me. Many afternoons, I was out at the Bible school grounds while the students made blocks or hauled dirt while I sat in the truck and studied for the next day's classes.

One time the parents of one of the students invited us all down to their ranch for a pig-killing day. This is a big occasion in Mexico in the small ranches and usually creates a festival spirit that lasts all day. The Mexican brother who was helping in the school, that truckload of students and I decided to drive down to this ranch for their special day. We picked up another brother who was supposed to show us how to get to the ranch, but it soon became obvious that he didn't know the way himself.

In Mexico, many people live in these out-of-the-way ranches who never own a vehicle, and the only way into the ranch is a trail where they ride their horses or walk or ride a bicycle. I didn't know it when we started on this particular "picnic," but the road into this ranch was one of those trails. First we took the road off the highway, but before long, it narrowed down to a trail over which horses and people only could travel. We continued anyway. (The students wanted to go.) We had to have a couple of the boys run along in front of the truck to look for big rocks and to warn me about holes up ahead. Finally, even the trail for the horses ran out and we were in the bushes. But we went ahead and made it to that ranch.

As we arrived, we noticed that there didn't seem to be much celebrating going on, so after visiting for a while, we asked the parents of the student who had made the original invitation, "When are we going to kill the pig?"

"Oh, we've already killed the pig," they answered.

"And the meat?" we asked.

"It's all gone, also. We've already eaten part of it and smoked the rest!"

I don't know what happened to that pig. I don't know if they really had already killed it, but I do know that we didn't get even a tortilla to eat out of that trip.

Then, there was the trip back to the highway. We had to go back through the same holes and gullies, across the same rocks, and one time, we found ourselves going across freshly plowed land, but we got back to the highway. We never tried going to anyone else's pig-killing party.

As I said, the victories were many, but there were some defeats that we'll never forget. The following story of a young girl named Engracia was one of the most saddening experiences of all our time in Mexico.

We had been going into the village of La Constancia about two years when we met Engracia. La Constancia is one of the most poverty-stricken villages we have ever worked in. To get to the home where the services were held, it was necessary to park the vehicle and walk along a rocky trail for about one mile. This place was a valley that at some time was filled with volcanic rock, so when I say rocky trail, I am talking about more than just a few rocks here and there. It was a trail of continuous rocks with a patch of ground appearing only occasionally.

As the Mexican brethren who were taking care of the service one day came around a turn in the trail, they found a young girl sitting on one of the larger rocks with her head on her knees, doubled over in pain. The little boy from the village who was walking along with them went over to where she was seated and asked, "Are you still here?"

When he was questioned about why he had asked that question, he told them this story:

Engracia was well-known to the neighbors in this village because she had some sort of attacks. They could hit her at any time, with no warning, and could keep her incapacitated for hours. That particular attack had hit her while she was on the trail early that morning, and she had been there for hours without being able to move. That was why the little boy made the comment about her still being there.

Since they were only a few yards from the house where the service was to be held and Engracia was still unable to move, the brother in charge of the group picked Engracia up and took her into the house. The minute he touched her, she began to scream with pain so severe that she was incoherent. But the lady of the house knew Engracia and understood immediately what she needed. They put Engracia on the bed, laid hands on her and prayed for her in the name of Jesus. She grew calm as they prayed for her, and the pain began to subside.

The following week when they returned to La Constancia for the service, Engracia was waiting for them, smiling. She was bathed, in clean clothes and feeling well. She had been free of the attacks since the week before, and she believed God had healed her.

In the weeks and months that followed, Engracia attended all the services and became a part of the neighborhood once again. She had been living in a one-room rock hut, about five feet high, alone. Her family didn't want her in their home because of her unexpected attacks, so she had been moved into that little hut to die. Now, however, Engracia was well again, and she began to make trips into Durango to see her brothers and their families. They received her well, just as long as she had no more attacks. She began to look healthy as she continued to seek the Lord and delve into the Word of God.

Then one day when we went for the service, Engracia wasn't there. The lady of the house said she had gotten married. As we questioned her, we discovered that she hadn't really gotten married but was living with a man who was virulently anti-evangelical and would not let her attend the services. Common-law marriages are popular in Mexico. To take the necessary blood tests, X-rays, secure the license and pay the judge to get married sometimes takes more money than the poor man will make in a month, so many people live together as man and wife and raise their children without ever legally being married. We knew one couple who lived together for twenty-two years and had eight children before legally getting married.

When they found out about her "getting married," the Christians went to Engracia to pray with her and counsel her. As a result, she was in the service the next week, but she had come only to tell us good-bye. She was leaving with her "husband" and wouldn't be seeing us again. As we were leaving the service, I took Engracia by the hand, and with tears in my eyes, said, "Engracia, God has been so very good to you!"

Bowing her head, she said, "I know, but..."

In the weeks that followed, we didn't hear any news of Engracia. Not long afterward, we closed that mission in La Constancia because the majority of the people who wanted the Gospel had moved into the city looking for work.

Months later, I ran into a man who visited that village from time to time, and I asked about Engracia.

"Oh," he said. "She's dead."

"Dead," I cried. "How did that happen?"

"Not long after she went off with that man, she began having those attacks again," he said. "As her condition worsened, the man left her, and before long, she was back in her hut, abandoned even by her own family."

"And she died alone?" I asked.

"Yes, she died alone," he answered.

What sadness! How my heart ached for Engracia. She had been so happy, so clean. Now she was gone. Forever. Surely we could have done more for Engracia.

Although their National Constitution guarantees their religious freedom, and there are laws to uphold that freedom, the Mexican Christians still cannot be assured of safety when there is opposition from the people. It all depends on the local officials. On one occasion, the mayor of a town sent out soldiers to protect some of our people from an angry crowd that was disrupting the service. But the following story is more the norm when it comes to religious persecution in some parts of Mexico.

Max was an elderly man who worked with us in a town called Montemorelos, fifteen miles from the city of Durango. He had been invited by one family to come to its home and preach. For a few weeks, the services progressed with no problem.

It was summer, and since my sister-in-law, Karen Witt, had come down especially to work in some Vacation Bible Schools, we decided it would be good to have a VBS in Montemorelos. Life in the villages can be pretty monotonous, and since the activities prepared were interesting, a good number of children attended that first session of classes.

The second day of VBS, Karen and her co-worker, Martha,

had left the car about one mile from the village because of the bad road. Walking the last mile into town, they were met at the entrance by a group of some two hundred angry women who were carrying clubs, bricks and sticks. Their purpose was to turn our two young girls around and prevent their having another day of VBS.

Karen tried to reason with the women, but they would not let them pass on into the village. So two sad young girls sang the praises of God all the way to the car they had left a mile down the road.

The next day, Karen and Martha got pastor Max and another American visitor to go back to Montemorelos with them so they would have some support in case the women were waiting for them again. They were. Only this time, there were some men in the crowd, and the men were carrying machetes.[20] This time Max talked to the people as the American young man stood at his back and off to one side. There was much screaming. The scene was one of confusion.

Suddenly, out of the corner of his eye, the American caught sight of a woman who was making her way slowly around behind Max. In her hand, she carried a machete. Stealthily, she crept up behind Max. Breaking into a run, she raised the machete over her head in preparation of bringing it down on Max's back. Moving with the urgency of life and death, the American young man yelled at Max and grabbed woman's arm at the same time. After this sobering act, the town's mayor was able to disperse the crowd shortly. However, he warned the evangelicals not to go into the town for the VBS classes again.

Once again, our group set out for the one-mile walk back to the vehicle it had left at the highway, praising God all the way.

We decided to let things cool off some in Montemorelos and not try to go in again for a while. After waiting a few weeks, Max made his way to the home of the family who had invited him to preach the Gospel. The family was fearful. After singing a couple of choruses and reading a few Scriptures, Max prepared to leave. But somehow word had gotten out, and as he stepped out the door of the house, the crowd of people was waiting for him again. Once again, the mayor of the town had to disperse them. This time, he walked with Max all the way to the entrance of the village to make sure he got out all right.

After waiting another short while to let things cool off, Max went into Montemorelos again to visit the family who had asked for the Gospel. This time, they were more fearful than ever. The people of the village were threatening to kill the family's cows and burn their crops. And as the man of the house said, "They are capable of doing it, too."

As before, when Max stepped out the door of this family's home, the crowd of people was there. Again, the mayor had to disperse the crowd and escort Max to the entrance of the village. Only this time the mayor told Max: "This is the last time. This makes three times I have saved your life and dispersed these people who want to kill you. No more. If you come in here again, and they want to kill you, they can kill you. I am not acting on your behalf anymore."

With that, he turned on his heels and walked back down the dusty road into his village.

Even though he had received official orders from the army in Durango, this mayor would go no further with these Evangelicals and refused them further protection. The family we were visiting became so fearful of the people's threats that they asked us to not return. And we didn't. There were too many other places where the people did want the Gospel, and it was to those places that we went.

Karen and Martha held some successful Vacation Bible Schools that summer, even though they continued to have to walk a lot and rough it in some primitive conditions in the villages. In one of the villages, there were so many scorpions in the fields, in the church and in the house where they were staying that Karen could hear them falling off the rafters over her head and landing on the floor every night.

Scorpions in the state of Durango are as feared as snakes. There is something in the mineral content of the soil and the water that makes some of them as deadly as rattlesnakes. There is a special unit in the state hospital that is used only for treating scorpion bites. The bite paralyzes the people and causes them to slowly asphyxiate. A small child is given only thirty minutes and an adult two hours to show the symptoms of asphyxiation unless they are given the antidote.

But Karen and Martha were brave. Despite the fact that they were living in the midst of all these creatures day and night, they made it through their five days of VBS in that little village, and many children who accepted Jesus for the first time in those classes are now adults and serving God. Some are in ministry.

The type of persecution we had encountered in Montemorelos and the problems with scorpions, bad roads, lack of electricity, etc., was accepted as coming with the terrain. We were taking the Gospel into areas that had never had it before, and there was going to be persecution. However, there was another type of persecution that was not expected and which caused more hurt and damage than any other: the persecution that came from our own brothers in faith.

One of those cases was with a man who had come down from the United States to work with us, but it wasn't long before he and the leaders of a major Protestant denomination in the city of Durango were working together to take over the works and missions that the Lord had helped us to raise up. In one of these places, we had already built a building, but these men told the people in that congregation that they should get a petition and tell Nola to "Get out and take her bricks with her."

Of course, the people in the congregation came straight to me and told me what had happened.

After looking at them for a few minutes, I asked them, "Do you want me to leave?"

"No! No!" they said.

"Because," I continued, "if you want me to leave, all you have to do is say so, and I'll leave. And I won't take my bricks with me."

But the people insisted they didn't want us to leave, so we continued holding services in that little town for several years.

That person also caused trouble in the Bible school and with people who were working with us in the missions. It was a constant round of talk, gossip and criticism. It brought a lot of hurt and confusion at a time when I didn't need any more emotional trauma.

Since my teen years, Isaiah 4:10 has been one of my favorite Bible verses: *"Fear thou not, for I am with thee; be not dismayed, for I am thy God: I will strengthen thee; yea, I will help thee; yea, I will uphold thee with the right hand of my righteousness."*

During all this gossip and criticism, I turned to this passage. But this time, I read through the next few verses: *"Behold, all they that were incensed against thee shall be ashamed and confounded; they shall be as nothing; and they that strive with thee shall perish. Thou shalt seek them, and shalt not find them, even them that contended with thee; they that war against thee shall be as nothing, and as a thing of naught. For I the Lord thy God will hold thy right hand, saying unto thee, Fear not; I will help thee."*

Wow! And that's what happened. A few months later, the person who was instigating nearly all the trouble left Mexico and moved back to the United States. When that happened, everything calmed down, and we were able to keep moving forward.

It had been nearly three years since Jerry's death and the workload was steadily increasing. Many times on Sunday, I would drive our pickup truck for eight hours straight going from village to village for the services.[21] One Sunday, I drove so much that my left arm and side went into some kind of constrictive cramp, and I couldn't even lift my arm. A friend had to drive me back to Durango that night. The doctor told me the next day that it was from exhaustion.

The reason for the exhaustion was that I struggled with fear, so there weren't many nights that I got eight hours of sleep. Sometimes, the girls who were staying with me would sit up with me until the wee hours of the morning, playing the radio and talking because I was afraid to go to sleep. Other times, I finally went to bed, but I slept with a pistol under my pillow. (I don't know what I would have done with the thing. It didn't have any bullets, and I didn't know how to shoot it.) I was having an inordinate number of headaches, which would sometimes last for a week before letting up. My heart was racing. Sometimes I felt sick, and I was alone. There were problems everywhere: with the Bible school students, with the pastors in the United States, with the help in the house and with the Mexican pastors themselves. Besides, my little boys were growing up and proving to be a hand full. I was afraid they'd get out of control. Mark and Philip went through a stage about this time where they climbed up on the top of our house and jumped off, using my umbrella as a parachute. Everywhere, there were problems. I was exhausted and could no longer cope with everything that was coming at me from so many directions.

I was afraid to go to sleep because someone might vandalize the car or the truck, or steal something out of my home, or break into our home during the night. But the biggest cause of all this fear was a situation for which I still have no explanation.

We were living in a big house at that time and had several young people who were down from the United States for the summer helping in different ways. Two of them were my brother, Buddy Holder, and my sister-in-law, Karen Witt. Karen was sleeping in the bedroom directly across the hall from me, and Buddy was sleeping in another part of the house that was accessible only through an outside door.

On that particular night, I went upstairs to bed before the others and asked that they be sure to lock everything up before going to bed. I awoke at 1:20 a.m., when one of my little boys was whining because the mosquitoes were biting him. The girl who helped me in the house, Lupita, and I spent a few minutes finding the insecticide to spray the boys' room and getting them settled back down for the remainder of the night. The open, winding stairway came almost to the doors of these three bedrooms where the boys, Karen and I were sleeping.[22] As I turned in the door of the boys' bedroom to go back to my own room, my hand was on the light switch, and I was facing down that open, curving staircase. Suddenly, I heard what sounded like someone dragging a heavy box across the floor downstairs. Thinking that someone had gotten into the house through one of the windows downstairs, I went into the bedroom where Karen was sleeping, flipped on her bedroom light and asked her if she and Buddy had locked the house.

"Yes, we did," she said.

"Are you sure?" I asked.

"Yes, I'm sure," she answered, not really happy about being given the third degree at that time of the morning.

I shrugged my shoulders and, with my hand on her light switch, turned toward my bedroom. The door of Karen's room faced directly downstairs, and as I stood there, I saw someone standing on the stairs. Having lived alone for some time now and having trained myself to be sure about every unexplained sound and sight before sounding any alarm, I looked at whatever it was that stood about halfway up the stairs. It was looking through a big window, which opened out to the part of the house where Buddy was sleeping. The light was still on in my bedroom across the hallway, so what I saw was not a shadow. It was a being. It had a definite shape, but I could not make out the distinct features. It was tall, and it was black. As I stood there with my hand still on the light switch, this thing turned on the stairs and looked at me. My mind raced as I tried to think of who it could be. It could not be Lupita because she was much shorter and had a long braid down her back. This thing appeared to be a man with short hair brushed straight back. And it was terribly black.

After I decided it wasn't Lupita, I thought maybe it was Buddy. But it couldn't be Buddy because he was sleeping in the other part of the house, and the only way he could have gotten in downstairs is if someone opened the door for him. No one had. As I stood watching and trying to decide whom this was, the thing was coming up the stairs toward me. I had trained myself so sternly not to panic and go hysterical at every little sound or sight that the thing was at the top of the stairs and only about three feet from me when I slammed the door to the bedroom—remember, I was still in Karen's room. Slamming that door was not something I decided to do or something I did voluntarily. I believe God slammed that door! I don't remember doing it, but the next thing I do remember, I was sitting on the floor of that bedroom leaning against the door, thinking that someone was going to push on the door and try to get into the bedroom. And I was screaming like I have never screamed in my life!

Karen came up out of the bed like a shot, crying, "What is it? What is it?"

"There's someone out there!" I screamed.

Not knowing what else to do, Karen ran to the window and began to shake the venetian blind, beat on the window and yell for Buddy. She said later that as she was shouting, she rambled in the closet trying to find an umbrella or something with which to hit the thing if it did come into the room. She came up with an old purse, and that was what she was holding in her hands while walking the floor and yelling at the top of her voice.

But, no one ever put even the slightest pressure on that door. By this time, I was a complete bowl of jelly, sitting on the floor, leaning against the door and having hysterics. If anyone had tried to push on that door and come in, they would have had no problem because I couldn't even stand up.

All this time, which couldn't have been more than a few minutes, Karen continued to beat on the window and yell for Buddy. Finally, we heard Buddy out in the back yard yelling for someone to come and open the door.

"I can't get in!" he yelled.

Lupita went down the stairs and opened the door so Buddy could get into the house. She said later that she didn't know what on earth had happened. She thought that maybe I had seen another mouse (there were quite a few around those days), but when the screaming and yelling continued, she didn't have an explanation. She had no qualms about going down the stairs and opening the door for Buddy.

By this time, every light in the house was on. Buddy searched the house—every nook and cranny. He could find no one, no sign of a visitor nor any indication that the outside door had been open. Finally he came back up the stairs and sat down beside me on the top stair. I literally couldn't make it any farther.

"Well," he said, "either it was your imagination, or it was a ghost."

"Buddy," I said, "it may have been a ghost, but it was not my imagination."

Years later, I was telling one of my younger sisters about this experience, and she told me that she'd had a similar one in that house when she came for Christmas one year with our mom and dad. She had sensed a restlessness in the house that night and had seen the shadow of a man's head in the window in the exact spot where I had seen this thing on the stairs that night.

Now, I don't believe in ghosts. I don't believe that the dead come back when they have died violent deaths and can't be put to rest. So this was not the explanation we needed. This happened at a time when there was already much persecution and confusion in the work, so I believe the enemy threw this little episode in to try to wipe us out completely.

It was after this that I had problems sleeping night after night. Many nights, I sat up listening to the radio until daybreak. In the daytime, I was all right and told myself that I was being ridiculous. But at night, that fear came back, and it was like it was trying to kill me. Sometimes I took my Bible to bed with me and went to sleep with my hands resting on it, claiming peace for that night's sleep. Incidentally, that worked better than anything. But it had gotten to the place where I was losing so much sleep that I was becoming ill. One day, I went down to the study and poured the whole thing out before the Lord. I wept, and I prayed. I had to have relief.

A few months after this happened, I was in Idaho at a Missions Conference and was asked to speak in one of the morning sessions. As I shared with the attendees what was happening in Mexico, I felt led to share also my sleeping problem. At the end of the service, Dorrlene Freeborn, a friend of mine, came up to me and told me that she had felt that burden of sleeplessness and lack of rest while I was talking.

"It was like I, myself, was experiencing the exhaustion because of the lack of sleep," she said. "Then, the Scripture in Psalm 4:8 came to mind, and I want to share that verse with you: *'I will both lay me down in peace, and sleep; for thou, Lord, only makest me dwell in safety.'* "

I began to take hold of that verse and make it mine. I was going to lie down in peace, and I was going to sleep because it was only in the Lord that I could live in safety. Again, the Word of God had supplied my need.

But God was moving in a special way again, and things were beginning to change. Big time.

8

All in God's Time

My spirit and my emotions were healing. It had been a long, difficult and painful process. But God had done the work.

Naturally, the thought that I might marry again had crossed my mind. For the first few years, I had been too busy recuperating and keeping the work organized and moving to do much more than think about it. A couple of years after Jerry's death, some friends invited me to visit them and to meet a young man whom they thought was just right for me. He was a prince of a fellow and a fine Christian, but it didn't take me long to realize that emotionally, I was not ready for marriage yet. Jerry was still too much a part of my make-up to be able to think about marrying just yet.

As time passed, several men presented their attentions, and I was variously shocked and amazed. One was in his sixties. Another one was a good man, but divorced, and I knew and liked his former wife. Some in Durango presented me with serenades and flowers. One afternoon, I came in from one of my trips out to the villages and found an enormous floral arrangement waiting for me. My baby-sitter said, "Mr. So and So sent it." Another time in the middle of the night, we were all awakened by the sound of musicians tuning up their guitars, violins, bass violins, etc. There was a full-size "mariachi" band in front of my house getting ready to serenade me. They were brought by the same man who sent the flowers. For at least an hour, they sang songs about thwarted love, incredible love, etc. I never opened the door or indicated in any way that I had even heard them, much less enjoyed the music. I could only imagine what the neighbors were thinking.

I don't mean that men were lined up at my doorsteps begging for the opportunity to share my affection. These things happened over a period of more than three years and on the whole were few and far between.

But I was beginning to pray about it. So were the boys. The third anniversary of Jerry's death rolled around, and my spirit was only beginning to be in condition to seriously consider remarriage. Little Jerry told me he was praying for the Lord to send him a daddy. A few weeks later, I asked him if he was still praying for God to send him a daddy, and he said, "No. I have already prayed, and the Lord knows I need a daddy."

The work was growing. The boys were growing. Both the boys and the work had gotten to the size and nature that I could no longer handle them. David and Rene were leaving to go to language school, so I was alone for the first time since Jerry's death. It was suggested that I leave Mexico for a while and go to the States. Perhaps there I would meet someone suitable. But I couldn't feel right about that, either. The work needed attention and help. So I continued to pray and work in the mission. I also continued to hold this thing before God.

I often tell my friends that there has never been a more hopeless case than mine. I was twenty-eight years old by now. I had three small children. I had a work in Mexico to look after. Jerry's memory was all around whoever might decide to come. Surely this was a case for the Lord, for in the natural, it was hopeless. But God sent the most eligible bachelor west of the Mississippi knocking on my front door.

For four months, I prayed earnestly about this. I really felt I could no longer continue the way things were. One night as I was kneeling beside my bed crying out to God about this, I felt an assurance in my spirit that He did have a companion for me. Naturally, I wanted to know right then who it was God had in mind. I began listing in my mind those who had been coming around to pay attention.

"Is it Jim?"

"No, it's not Jim."

"Is it Bob?"

"No."

"Is it Kenneth?"

"No."

After calling off a few more names and the answer still being, "No," I finally asked in frustration, "Well, if it's not any of these, then who is it?"

And the answer came back, "Frank Warren."

I was so surprised that I sat upright and laughed. I had never even met Frank Warren. *Well,* I thought, *if this is of God, it will come to pass. If it's not, I will not worry about it.*

In June of that year, my brother, Buddy Holder, came down for a short visit, having just left a camp in Shreveport, Louisiana. After I picked him up at the bus station and we were driving to that night's service, Buddy suddenly asked me, "Do you know Frank Warren?"

"No," I said. "But from what I have heard, he must be a fine person."

I didn't tell him about what had happened while I was praying a few weeks earlier.

Nodding his head, Buddy said, "I think he is interested in you."

(Frank has no idea what he said or did that caused Buddy to think he might be interested in me. He had never met me and only knew what he had heard through the grapevine. He thought I had five children. He said when he first heard about me, he wondered what kind of weird lady would try to raise five children by herself in Mexico.)

"Anyway," Buddy continued, "he's coming down to Mexico with a group of people from Shreveport this coming month, and several of them want to go to Durango and visit the work there. They asked me to make the arrangements for them to be in some kind of services with you while they are in Mexico."

Arrangements were made for Pastor Keeling and Frank

Warren to come to Durango and minister to some of the pastors there and preach in the city of Durango. Within a few weeks, they were in Durango, in my home, and ministering in the churches.

FRANK TELLS HIS STORY

Frustrated would be the best word to describe my situation. For twelve years, I had felt the call of God upon my life. For nine years, I had been making trips on my summer vacations to Mexico with a ministry team. Coming home from those trips was the beginning of part of my frustration. The call to missionary work was upon my life, but God would not give me direction. After much prayer and crying out, year after year, the heavens were silent on the issue. This was part of my frustration.

After coming to the Lord at age twenty-two, I made the selection of a wife a spiritual decision. I knew whom I married would affect future ministry. I was determined to let God have the last word on this subject. This was easy for a few years, but after God kept telling me "no, no, no," it became another frustration in my life. I was frustrated about the call of God and about being a bachelor already moving into my mid-thirties.

Then, in June 1967, God did a wonderful thing. Because of the frustration of going to Mexico every year and coming home with a strong desire to go to the mission field and getting no direction from God, I decided to go see my Uncle Ernest in North Carolina one year and forget about the trip to Mexico. God had other plans. As the time for the trip to Mexico drew nearer, my friend who headed up the trips to Mexico called me concerning the plans for the trip, and before I knew what was happening, I was on my way to Mexico again.

Our destination was Torreon, with part of the group going on to Durango for three days to be with a lady named Nola Witt. Nola was a widow and, from what I had heard, had five kids. I later found out there were only three kids. I had thought, What kind of creature is that? After some confusion about who would be in the team going to Durango, I found myself in the group and along with Nola's brother, Buddy Holder, knocking on Nola's front door in Durango.

In Durango, I stayed pretty much in the background. Nola talked quite a bit with Pastor Keeling, who she said reminded her of her dad. During those three days, something broke loose inside of me. I found myself in love with that beautiful creature and her three boys. I was raised with a house full of girls, and the thought of having some boys in the house was appealing, as was the thought of having Nola as my wife.

It wasn't a whirlwind romance. It was a deliberate, planned romance, guided by the Holy Spirit and executed at maximum velocity. After arriving back home in Shreveport and realizing these feelings I was having were real, I shot off a letter to Nola. Before the letter had time to get to Durango, I felt strongly impressed to call her. The message I was receiving in my spirit was, "Boy, get the lead out of the seat of your pants. This is it." So I made the call to Durango, and the excitement I picked up on the other end of the line gave me great encouragement and joy.

In those days, I spent a lot of time listening to a record Nola had made and day dreaming. One of my favorite songs on that record was "I Asked the Lord to Comfort Me," and I was hoping to be part of the answer to that prayer. I still don't know why the company I worked for at that time didn't fire me. I made many errors in the accounting part of my job because in the middle of the day's work, I mentally ran off to Durango.

My sisters, excited about the possibility of their bachelor brother (now thirty-five years old) getting married, helped lay the first plan of attack. Nola was invited by one of my sisters who had met her years before in Bible College to be her house guest for a few days on Nola's trip to Georgia to visit her parents. My mother was the only one with any reservations. Behind my back, she told the girls, "Since

Frank has been back from Mexico, all I hear is, 'Nola this and Nola that.' " After meeting Nola and her boys, she capitulated, and in the end, if I hadn't married Nola, I think she and my dad would have run me off.

On July 12, 1967, just three weeks after meeting Nola, I picked her and the boys up at the train station and whisked them over to my sister's house. After eating supper and putting the boys to bed, Nola and I had our first moments together—except for fifteen minutes alone we'd had in Mexico when she went with me to fill the car up with gasoline. Twelve years before that, I had made a decision that the next girl I kissed would be the girl I would marry. I finally got my kiss. Later, Nola said she didn't doubt one minute that it had been twelve years since I had kissed anyone, but that I was improving.

The next morning, I picked Nola and the boys up for a luncheon engagement with some friends. About 5 a.m. that day, I had awakened and felt a strong urge to get a little proposal speech together. So when I picked them up for the luncheon, I cornered Nola in a room in my sister's house and delivered my brief proposal: "You don't have to give me an answer right now, but I want you to know that I love you and want to marry you." I didn't get an answer, but I was still feeling good about everything. On the way over to our friend's home, Jerry (then seven years old) leaned over from the back seat and asked, "Frank, are you coming to Durango to be our Daddy?" I said, "What did you say, Jerry?" I wanted to hear him say that again. He repeated the question, and I said that it sounded like a good idea to me. I was so glad I had just proposed to Nola. I was getting encouragement from all sides.

One week later, I was in Marietta, Georgia, with a set of rings. I arrived late Saturday, and after visiting with Nola for a while, I went over to spend the night at the home of Nola's sister and her husband. All I heard that night was how great Jerry (Nola's first husband) was. They talked about how he liked to hunt and showed me one of his guns.

They talked about how big he was, especially the size of his hands. It was evident the great love they had for Jerry, and maybe in a subtle way, they were telling me I could never take his place. The next day, my future mother-in-law used the more direct approach. When I mentioned to her that I would like her approval concerning marrying Nola, she burst into tears and replied, "Well, just don't think you can take Jerry's place." Later, I realized that my mother-in-law's loyalties run deep and she became just as loyal to me as she had been to Jerry. But on that Sunday morning in Marietta, nothing could have deterred me from my determination to marry Nola. My thinking was, Great. Let's talk about Jerry. After all, I wanted to marry Nola and help raise his kids. God was doing a wonderful thing. I was taking my place in the future of this family and the work in Mexico.

Nola had not given me a "Yes" answer, but she hadn't said "No," either. She kept telling me I didn't know her. My answer was, "I don't care, I still want to marry you." She was right, and I was right. I discovered later that she had waited to give me her answer until she saw how her family reacted, and now we knew that her family approved. We were engaged on the 21st of July, one month from the date we had met. That night, I persuaded her to give me a date for the wedding. She set the 21st of October.

On October 21, 1967, a book was closed on my life of bachelorhood, along with all its frustrations of waiting and waiting for the activating of the call of God upon my life. God did a wonderful thing that day, and has been doing wonderful things ever since.

★★★★★★★★★★★★★★★★★

Interestingly enough, the first person I ever heard speak Frank Warren's name was none other than Jerry himself. Soon after we were married and Jerry was still in Bible College, Frank's younger sister, Barbara, was in Jerry's class. Jerry was talking about her one day as we ate lunch and said that her brother, Frank, was coming down to take her back home to Shreveport for the weekend. After that, from time to time, his name would come to my attention, but I never met him. One time after I was a widow and was visiting the IBC campus, I stood on the steps of the girls' dormitory and watched him open the door for a friend of mine that he was taking out on a date. There was a "mystery" about Frank. He was handsome, a strong Christian and a responsible man who treated everyone with courtesy. No one could understand why he had never married. Here he was thirty-five years old and didn't even have a steady girlfriend.

Knowing that Frank was to be part of the group that was visiting, I was on edge. Meeting him for the first time, I agreed, he was handsome! He was six feet tall, and he had greenish/gray eyes, light brown hair and the perfect Grecian profile. Besides that, he lifted weights and could do 72 push-ups without stopping and was therefore muscular in his upper body.

From the beginning, Frank sought me out. He sat next to me at meals, he rode with me when we went somewhere together, and whenever either of us would come into the room where the other was located, our eyes would meet and there were messages flying back and forth. Everyone in the group was tremendously excited. Most of them had known Frank for years, and they found it almost unbelievable that Frank was finally interested in a member of the opposite sex. As I lay on the top bunk in my boys' bedroom one morning, I could hear Frank and Pastor Keeling talking in the living room. Excited by what was developing and hoping this was "the real thing," I told the Lord that if this really was of Him, then please make it move smoothly. I was not of an age or a frame of mind to have one of those rocky, emotionally exhausting courtships. On his last night in Mexico, he asked me to ride with him to the gas station to fill up his car in preparation for the trip the next day. Not knowing exactly what to expect, but knowing that something was definitely in the air, I went with him. Frank is probably the best gentleman I have ever dated. Although his face positively glowed that night whenever he looked at me, and my face was glowing back at him, he still only asked permission to write to me when he got back to Louisiana. Actually, I was a little disappointed. Maybe his friends were right when they told me that even if Frank did decide he wanted to court me, he would take a long time to get things moving. He had the reputation of moving cautiously.

But that's not the way it worked out. By the time he left Mexico, everyone knew something was in the air and his face lit up like a Christmas tree whenever I walked into the room. Within a few days after he left, I was receiving nice letters and long, expensive telephone calls from Frank. When he had been visiting us in Durango, I gave him a photograph of myself with the three boys. One Sunday afternoon when he called, he said he had been studying that picture, and the thought came to him that he must be crazy to think there would ever be a place for him in that picture. But, I assured him quickly, that we all felt he would fit into the picture just perfectly.

I was excited. And happy. And responsive. It amazed me that something about which I had prayed so earnestly for so long could be happening. Frank was very sought after by the single ladies in the church. He was the right age, the right disposition, and besides all that, he loved Mexico and my boys.

Frank says that the first Sunday after he got back to Shreveport, he was lying on the carpet in his bedroom thinking about me, when he felt a strong urge to call me in Durango. He immediately called, and after hanging up, he heard a little voice telling him, "This is it. You'd better quit dragging your feet and get moving." And did he ever get moving! Telephone calls, letters, flowers, pictures, the works! We began a long-distance courtship that only lasted a few weeks. Although it seemed that God had taken a while to answer our prayers, once He began to move, everything was racing along at a dizzying speed. Less than one month after we met, Frank proposed, and within three months after that, we were married. This was from a man everyone thought was a "confirmed" bachelor and didn't really want to get married. Frank always said that when you've prayed as long as he had about getting married, when the answer finally came, he didn't see any reason for wasting any more time.

One of my most vivid memories of Frank's first visit to Durango was one afternoon as he sat in an armchair in my living room. My baby, Philip, was three-and-one-half years old by this time, and he had turned to Frank in an unusual way. Philip went running across the room toward Frank with his arms outstretched and jumped up into Frank's arms and onto his lap, giving him a hug as he did so. There was instant love on both sides. Frank says that he fell in love with the boys before he fell in love with me.

That was another frustration in Frank's life. He had never been in love. He had just about made up his mind that love was something that happened to other people. He decided he would just find himself a good dedicated Christian girl and forget about falling in love. He also had decided that the only way he was going to be able to go to the mission field was to get a job with an oil company or something (he was an accountant) and go to South America. Maybe that way, he could finally get involved in mission work. Then he made that fateful trip to Durango.

Before I told Frank I would marry him, the boys and I went to Shreveport to meet his family. Driving from Durango to Shreveport, we stopped in San Antonio and spent the night on the campus of International Bible College, where Rev. David Coote was president. It seemed everyone on campus knew about the "thing" between Frank and me, and since President Coote had always been such a special friend to both Jerry and me, he came over to the apartment where I was staying on campus and wanted to talk about Frank. He had known Frank even longer than his friends in Shreveport.

"You know," he said, "that Frank is not the same type of personality that Jerry was. Jerry had an outgoing, effervescent personality and was the type of person who was always looking for another adventure. You need to take all that into consideration before you become seriously involved with Frank. It's not fair to him to expect him to be another Jerry."

"President Coote," I said, "I feel I've had enough adventure to last me two more lifetimes. I don't need any more adventure. I need someone who is steady, dependable and who loves God as well as me and the boys. I believe Frank is the man."

The boys and I took the train from San Antonio to Shreveport and arrived there late at night. Frank already had decided he wanted to marry me, and that night after he picked the boys and I up at the train station, we went to his sister's house, where we were going to be staying. Before leaving, Frank asked me if it would be all right for him to kiss me good night. I was amazed. I'd never been asked by anyone for permission to kiss me. I was afraid that if I said "yes," he would think I was being forward, but if I said "no," I would be lying. I decided that lying would be worse than being forward, so I said, "Yes!"

I didn't know it then, but Frank had made a pact with himself almost twelve years before that he would not kiss another girl until he found the one he was to marry. I told him later that after he kissed me that night, I truly believed him when he told me it had been twelve years since he had kissed anyone. It has to go down in history as one of the most poorly executed kisses ever. But things improved rapidly.

Frank was at his sister's the next morning to take the boys and I over to a friend's house for lunch. I was trying to get ready to leave and had my hair in a mess trying to arrange it when Frank came into the room where I was and said he had something he wanted to talk to me about.

Nervous and actually shaking, he said, "I just want you to know that I am in love with you and as far as I'm concerned, I want to marry you!" Talk about original proposals. But he was definitely off hold. He also had decided there was such a thing as falling in love. And things were moving fast. On the way over to the friend's house for lunch that day, Jerry put his arm around Frank's neck and asked, "Frank, are you coming to Mexico to be our daddy?" Frank was so thrilled with that question that he had Jerry repeat it several times.

Still, I didn't tell Frank I would marry him. Not that there was any doubt. I knew I would marry him, but I wanted to talk to Mom and Dad before making it official. After we left Shreveport, the boys and I went to Georgia, where the majority of my family lived. As we got onto the plane for the flight to Atlanta, Frank gave me an enormous corsage made of American Beauty pink miniature roses. It was beautiful. I was so happy I kissed Frank right there in front of his brother-in-law.

My family had already heard about Frank through Buddy, so they were expecting some sort of news when the boys and I arrived. It was a source of great joy to my mom and dad that I, at twenty-eight years old, wanted to talk to them before getting engaged.

Frank drove over in a few days and was with us in Marietta for a special day of celebration at the church. That afternoon as everyone was visiting and eating lunch together, Frank asked me again to marry him. And this time, I gave him an answer: Yes! That night as we were all eating pizza together, Frank pulled a calendar out of his wallet, laid it down in front of me and said, "Pick a date." I was thinking about something in maybe another year, when we could become better acquainted. But not Frank. He said he had waited long enough. So we set a date for three months later.

That trip to Georgia and his visit with my family would have stopped Frank in his tracks if it had been possible. My family had loved Jerry dearly, and although they didn't mind my remarrying, they wanted Frank to understand that Jerry had been special and that no one would ever take his place. He stayed with my sister and her husband, and his entire visit, my brother-in-law kept talking about Jerry: about the size of his hands, about how much he loved hunting, about things that had happened on his last visit. That same sister stood on the steps of the church that Sunday night and told Frank, "You're either the best man in the world or the craziest." She was referring to his desire to marry me and raise those boys. That afternoon after I told Frank I would marry him, he went to my mother.

"Mrs. Holder," he said, "I guess you know that Nola and I are planning to be married, but we both really do want your blessing."

My mother burst into tears and said, "All right. But don't think you can take Jerry's place."

I was amazed when I heard she said that. But my mom's loyalties run deep, and something about Frank's asking for her blessing moved her, and she's been his great friend ever since. Now she feels loyalty toward Frank.

The boys were in school, and Bible school classes were in session, so we decided to have the wedding in Durango. Since the engagement was official in July and the wedding wasn't until October, we decided that I would have to go to Durango to keep things going there and to plan the wedding. Frank's sister, Barbara, decided to go with me. In three weeks' time, I was to be back in Shreveport for an open house type of wedding shower for Frank and me, so Barbara was with me to make the trip back up.

We left Durango to go back to Shreveport in the late afternoon on the regular bus that went to Laredo, Texas. About half the trip was normal, and things went well. However, about halfway to Laredo (Saltillo-Monterrey area) we ran into Hurricane Beulah. Hurricane Beulah was one of the area's most historic hurricanes, and people still remember when it came in from the Gulf of Mexico and swept up through Monterrey and Saltillo and that part of Mexico. When we got to Saltillo, the bus stopped. All the highways were closed because of flooding and mudslides. Barbara and I knew that Frank had driven down to San Antonio to pick us up, but we had no way of letting him know that we were stranded in Saltillo. Frantically, we began looking for another way to get through. There were no commercial flights out of Saltillo, and the buses weren't running, so we had to try the train. It was pouring rain, the streets were flooded, and we had to get from the bus station to the train station to see what could be done. It was dawn, cold and wet. We waded in water almost to our knees to get to the taxi and then again to get from the taxi to the train station.

At the train station, they told us that some of the trains were still running, but not the one to Monterrey. We decided to take a train that was heading north away from the hurricane-ravaged area and have Frank pick us up there instead of in San Antonio. Somehow, we got word to Frank, and he drove down to Eagle Pass, Texas, where we were supposed to be arriving by train.

Mexican trains—even in the best of circumstances—are no joy ride. Especially the common type of stop-at-every-ranch train that we took. It was supposed to take nine hours to go from Saltillo to Eagle Pass. It took nineteen hours. And although the train did finally move out of the hurricane area, for the first half of the trip, we were still very much in the hurricane area. We hadn't gone thirty minutes when we had to stop. We sat there on the tracks for four hours before the train began to creep along again. This happened several times that day. Barbara and I were in the last car of the train, and at one point, two of the conductors came running back through the car toward the little platform that was on the back. (There was no caboose). Later when we asked the conductor what had happened, he said that as the train was moving across one of the bridges, it began to give away, and as the last car moved across the bridge, it had buckled and been destroyed. The reason the train kept stopping along the way was because a dam had broken nearby, and big stretches of the track were under water.

There was no food other than chips and sodas on the train. We were supposed to get into a particular town in time to get something to eat, but by the time we got there, it was so late that everything was closed. When we left Durango, Barbara and I hadn't thought to bring a sweater—after all, the sun was shining in Durango—and all day on that train, we shivered. We pulled clothes out of our suitcases trying to stay warm. I even tore apart a *Time* magazine I had with me and spread it over my upper body to stay warm. Some of the train windows were cracked, and the rain we were going through was so heavy that it penetrated those cracks and other loose places and wet the inside of the car. At one point, I had gone to sleep with my head resting against one of those windows, and when I woke up, my pillow was soaked and water was running down the inside of the window.

The conductor kept telling us, "Just a little more time. Just a little more time," but by the time it had been fifteen or sixteen hours, we were exhausted. We had no food or water and no bathrooms. Finally, only about an hour out of Eagle Pass, it began to tell on Barbara. She had been a tremendous sport in Durango and even on this miserable trip, but about the last couple of hours, she ran out of grace.

In tears, she said, "We're not ever going to get there. And even if we do, Frank won't be there to pick us up."

"Come on, Barbara," I said. "You've done great. This is just a little test of your faith."

"Test of my faith, nothing!" she said. "This is the trial of my life."

That made us both laugh, and we were able to face the last hour of that trip through Hurricane Beulah.

Frank was waiting anxiously for our arrival. When we saw him, it was like we had arrived in a safe harbor after a long time in a terrible nightmare. I don't think there has ever been a more welcome sight in my life than his smiling face and his open arms. He had brought a friend from San Antonio to show him the way to this little out-of-the-way Texas town, so Frank and I were able to sit in the back seat of the car and let his friend drive us back to San Antonio. I was happy to be able to turn the responsibility for the rest of this trip over to someone else. I laid my head in Frank's lap and slept nearly the entire trip back to Shreveport.

We barely made it to the open-house reception/wedding shower we were headed for in Shreveport. It was a great success.

By the time Frank got to Durango a few days before the wedding, we had guests stacked everywhere possible. Since all of the out-of-town guests were American and could speak no Spanish, they were unable to help with any of the wedding preparations. When we went to get the marriage license a few days before the wedding, we learned that they required a copy of Jerry's death certificate to prove that I was indeed a widow. I didn't have a copy of it. They had all been turned over to different government agencies and insurance companies. So two days before the wedding, Frank had to make a 160-mile round trip to Sombrerete, Zacatecas, to get a copy of the death certificate. I was still teaching at the Bible school every day and couldn't go with him.

Early the morning of the wedding, I was out in the fields of a flower farm picking flowers for the wedding. My mother was to arrange them sometime that day. Later that morning, Frank and I, along with six witnesses, were at the courthouse waiting for the judge, who was to conduct the civil ceremony. In Mexico, the only way to be legally married is to go before a civil judge. If a person wants a church wedding, that's fine, but the legal ceremony must be before the judge.

Even though we had an appointment, the judge was running very late. We waited in his office for three hours before he finally showed. That civil ceremony threw my tight scheduled off, and it never did recuperate. The first wedding made the second wedding late.

Yes, I was late for my own wedding. But, only thirty minutes. The real delay in the wedding came when I arrived at the church and found that the wedding music was lost. Nobody knew where it was. Altogether, we lost another hour while a friend went back to the house to look for the music. He couldn't find it. By this time, I was nearly hysterical. Sarah, Frank's sister, was directing the wedding, and it was at this point that she said firmly: "Everybody line up. This wedding is starting now, with or without music."

My little sister, Becky, was able to play the wedding march from memory, so our long-delayed wedding finally began. Three ministers preached and conducted the ceremony in two languages. My dad gave me away. Sarah says that before the wedding started, every one of the two hundred or so people attending got up and went outside at least twice during that long wait. But no one left.

In some cases of remarriage, there is a situation where the person cannot talk about their former spouse for fear of offending the current marriage partner. Especially in a case like mine could a situation like this be delicate. Here was a man coming down to continue a work that had been begun by his wife's former husband. Then there were the three boys who looked enough like their father to remind anyone of the facts. But neither Frank nor his family have ever demonstrated a spirit of jealousy in this situation. Frank has never shown the least bit of envy over Jerry's memory. In fact, many of Jerry's close friends have now become Frank's close friends, including Jerry's mother and father.

Nearly three years after we were married, our twin daughters were born in Durango. Frank kept saying in the months before their birth, *"God is able to do abundantly above all we can ask or think."* The doctor suspected that there might be two babies, but I did not believe it. After all, those things run in families, and as far as I knew, there had never been any twins in my family. But from the moment twins were suggested, Frank grabbed onto that thought and began saying "There are two!" He came into a room where the boys were playing and hold up two fingers and say "Two!" And the boys would laugh and clap their hands. On the day we had X-Rays taken to prove this thing one way or the other, the boys were out in the car waiting for the results. Naturally, the X-Rays showed two babies. So Frank walked to the front of the clinic and, without saying a word, held up two fingers and the boys went wild! With all the clapping, shouting and laughing, you would have thought they had just won the World Cup. We were all asking for one little girl, and God gave us two. Frances Lorene (Lorie) and Nola Jeanne (Jeannie) were born some twenty minutes apart in a small medical clinic above the post office in Durango. There was a relaxed atmosphere—so relaxed that Frank watched part of the surgery by peeking through the swinging doors that went into the operating room. There was an obstetrician, a general practitioner, a midwife, an anesthesiologist, a pediatrician and three nurses in attendance. The twins were overdue, so the doctors decided to do a Caesarean Section. It was a time in my life that I felt I was completely at the mercy of the Lord. I was in His hands. And it turned out well. When it was known that the second baby was also a girl, it was like a cheer came from that operating room, "Dos mujercitas!" (two little women). The arrival of our Lorie and Jeannie was a special blessing from God on our lives and helped to bind all seven of us together as never before.

This was the working of our omnipotent God. I could not have married a man who made me fearful to even speak Jerry's name. Jerry's life and testimony are a vital part of my own spiritual make-up. He had a part in my life that can never be replaced. He moved us to Mexico and started this work. Just because God chose to take him home is by no means a reason that his name should be eliminated from everyone's vocabulary. And it hasn't been. Frank never tried to replace Jerry. Frank simply came in and made his own place in our hearts. God knew that the boys and I needed someone who would be understanding when it came to Jerry's memory and what he had meant to us. He knew that it had to be someone who was big enough to be humble. And God chose well.

When Frank was getting ready to leave Louisiana for that last move down to Mexico, a minister friend of his said: "Just think, he is taking on marriage, three children and the mission field all at one time. Frank Warren is the only person I know who is man enough for the job."

Through the years, different people have asked what kind of father Frank has been to the boys. I'll answer that question by telling the following two stories.

My son Jerry Jr. was four years old at the time of Jerry's death. He was the one who had prayed most earnestly for the Lord to send him a daddy. Years later when this child was an adult and married himself, both he and his wife came back to Durango for a visit after having been in the United States for a few months. His wife, Vicky, told me that when they woke up that first morning back, they could hear Frank downstairs talking to someone. She said Jerry looked at her and said, "How good it is to wake up in the morning and hear my dad's voice."

The other story happened while all the boys were still at home. The port city of Mazatlan is only 180 miles from where we live, and we took the entire family over for a few days' vacation from time to time. The boys had become strong, confident swimmers, and they, along with Frank, thoroughly enjoyed body surfing in the Pacific Ocean. One year on one of these trips, Mark got too far out and was caught up in a riptide. He was so near the shore that none of the rest of us even noticed he was in distress until he caught Jerry's attention. So Jerry went out to try and help him. That made two of them in the riptide, and they were unable to get back alone. The boys got Frank's attention, and he went out to help them. Because of his years in the U.S. Navy, Frank knew more about water than the rest of us, and he knew that if he could get the boys up on the surface of the water instead of trying to swim that the wave action would take them to shore. So after much struggling and work, Frank got Jerry and Mark to lay on top of the water, and the waves brought them in to shore.

Philip, the twins and I had been sitting on the beach watching and not knowing what was happening until they all came out of the water, and Mark literally collapsed on the sand in front of me. He was shaking all over, his lips blue and his teeth chattering. That was when Frank told me what had happened.

Later as we all drove down the highway toward the restaurant where we were going to eat dinner, we passed the place on the beach where this had taken place. Mark was still in a daze, and as he stared out the car window at that place, he said, "Just think. I could be dead by now." It made a marked impression on his mind.

Jerry and Mark both believe that Frank saved their lives. Frank confided to me that there had been a time out there in the water when he wasn't certain he was going to be able to get both of the boys and himself back in to shore.

"But before leaving them out there alone, I would have died right there with them," he said.

Yes, God chose well.

EPILOGUE

A few months after Jerry and I arrived in Durango for the first time, we received a letter from a pastor friend of ours. "Keep your chin up," it said, "and keep trusting in God *because down the road of faith, there will be many surprises."*

And what surprises there have been! Some of them good, and some of them not so good. One of the good surprises has been the way God has fulfilled the original vision of raising up churches and missions in the area surrounding our location in the city of Durango. Through the years, one by one, God has raised up churches in the states of Durango, Zacatecas, Coahuila, Sinaloa and the Federal District, Mexico City. All of the churches are fulfilling the three "selfs" of effective missionary work: self-supporting, self-governing and self-propagating. As new missions open up, they are being cared for by a "mother" church in its area. Some thirty to thirty-five churches have been raised up in this manner.

Another part of the original vision was that of having a Bible school where the pastors, teachers and leaders who would be needed for these churches could be trained in the Word of God so they could return to their churches and become leaders in their own areas. This vision also has been fulfilled. Hundreds of people have gone through the Bible school and are now in positions of leadership such as pastor, deacon, worship leader, Sunday school teacher, youth leader and women's leader in their local congregations.

One of the surprises that we have encountered as we've walked down that road of faith was not a pleasant one: Jerry's death. So many people have commented about the tragedy of his death at such a young age. And it was a tragedy. Others question the wisdom of God concerning the need for Jerry to continue to live and fulfill the plan God had for his life. But I believe Jerry fulfilled the plan God had for his life.

Jerry was one soldier in an enormous war that is raging around us all the time. He gave his life in this war, but even as he fell, God already had others lined up to take his place. As the war continues to rage around us, some of those soldiers that are in the battle as a result of Jerry's life and testimony continue the same battle in which Jerry was engaged.

Remember Trini, the little girl who was in her home village that morning when the blue and white airplane dropped the Gospels of St. John from the air? Remember her aunt, who hid the Gospels from the religious authorities in her village? A visit to that town shows that today, it is a small community with fewer than one thousand residents. It is located in the high plain area of the state of Zacatecas, where little rain falls. The wind blows constantly, and as a person attempted to go from one building to the other, dust whipped into his face, and the cutting bite of the wind and the dust made it impossible to see where he was walking. That day, pausing for a few minutes, a person held a scarf over his face and tried to move forward to the buildings where the meeting was to be held that afternoon. Finally arriving at the destination, it was a shock to find that the small building was packed with believers who were enthusiastically singing the praises of Almighty God. Their faces were covered with the same dust that blinded the visitor. Their hair was full of the dust, their clothes were full of the dust—their entire lives are affected by the wind and dust of their small town. Their feet were encased in an apparatus called a "huarache," which is nothing more than a piece of tread from an old tire with leather straps tying the sandal-like device across their feet and around their ankles. Their feet are weather-beaten and cracked from years of working in the fields, the sun and the dust. But their sun-burned faces glow with the presence of God.

This little town received the Gospel for the first time that morning in April 1964 when Jerry Witt passed over their village and left them several copies of the Gospel of St. John. Not everyone received the Gospel with open hearts, but Aunt Tila did. She had been sick for a long time that morning the Gospel came into her life, and she used that Word of God that came into her life to claim healing for her body, and God healed her at the same time she received Him as her only Savior. Aunt Tila became the moving force behind the work of the Gospel in her town. She knocked on the doors of her neighbors and friends. She testified to her relatives. Many people rejected her, but she persisted in telling them about what God had done for her. Tila's uncle was a strong leader in the religious opposition in her town, and he led waves of persecution against these "upstart" evangelicals that were trying to change their old religion. There were chants and jeers. They ostracized the believers. But Aunt Tila continued speaking the truth of God's Word. This uncle went so far as to build an altar to one of his saints out in the street in front of his house, and they held parties with music and dancing and lots of food and, of course, lots of beer, all the time vilifying and ridiculing the new believers in town. There were mobs that would gather against the believers and stone them as they came out of their church where they had gathered.

But Aunt Tila continued to speak the truth, and the day finally came when this uncle of hers became a believer. He tore down his altar and destroyed his idols. Today that uncle is a strong Christian and one of the leaders in the small congregation in that town.

Although the congregation is small today, that's not because of its lack of influence. The surrounding area has been evangelized since that fateful day in 1964, and dozens of people who came to know Jesus through that one small "light" that shone brightly have moved into other areas because of their jobs and are no longer a part of that town.

That small village was Trini's home, and when she was thirteen years old, a missionary came to her town and invited everyone out to see the movie "I Beheld His Glory." She already had accepted the Lord Jesus by this time, but that movie was a confirmation in her spirit, and immediately after that, she also moved out of the village and went into a larger town to serve God. There she met a missionary from Puerto Rico, and today, she is the wife of the pastor of a thriving church in their city.

One man fell in battle, but dozens of others have been raised up to take his place.

Another of the surprises that God has blessed us with is the way a good number of people were challenged to give their own lives to the work of the mission field as a result of Jerry's testimony and death.

Jerry and Sandy Owens were a young couple from Bloomington, Illinois, who had just begun to attend a church where Jerry Witt had visited when they were exposed to their first missionary conference. They were stirred personally to hear the stories, to see pictures of people from different lands and talk to the missionaries personally about the work they were doing. Jerry Witt had challenged their pastor and the congregation to hold this and other missionary conferences.

Not long after this, Jerry Witt was killed.

The time came around for the second missionary conference, and the story that was impacting all their lives was the story of Jerry's death. The song they were all singing during this time was the song that had meant so much to Jerry and which had been sung at his funeral: "Souls are crying, men are dying...Go out and win them..." Jerry and Sandy could see those souls dying and going into eternity without Christ. It put tears in their eyes, a dryness in their throats and a great desire in their hearts to help these people know Jesus. Again and again, they could hear those souls crying and see those souls dying.

Jerry and Sandy felt they were doing their part for world missions. They were giving financially and praying. Giving to missions hadn't been difficult for them, and after all, what more could be expected from a young couple that was living from paycheck to paycheck? But every night during this second missions conference, they rushed home from work, rushed to the church and sat with their eyes glued to the front of the church as they traveled to far-away places by way of slides and the stories of the missionaries. They heard again about how Jerry had been killed in the mountains of Mexico and about how there was a need for more missionaries. They heard about a young man with three small children who had paid the ultimate price for taking the Gospel message to the poor mountain people of Mexico. His name was Jerry Witt, and Jerry Owens' name just happened to be "Jerry" also. Jerry Owens felt he was getting to know Jerry Witt in his spirit, even though he had already gone on to be with the Lord. Before that conference was over, Jerry and Sandy Owens had a long talk. They had to respond to this need that had been presented through the life and testimony of Jerry Witt.

They went to Bible College in San Antonio, and it was there that they met Nola. On several occasions, she sang and spoke during the chapel services. There was something that drew Jerry and Sandy to Nola. Their hearts went out to her as she tried to raise those three small boys and carry on the mission work at the same time.

As students at Bible College, they were challenged to pray over certain areas of the world during their missions prayer meetings. Jerry found himself kneeling with the map in front of him and wondering where the Lord was going to send him and Sandy. How in the world were they going to know where they should go? Then one day in chapel, a young man from Guatemala spoke, and God began to speak to their hearts. Not long after that, they were talking to Nola about missions, and she said to Sandy and Jerry completely out of the blue: "When Jerry was alive, we talked about going to Guatemala some day and starting a work there. Maybe that's where you and Sandy should go." Jerry didn't think that was the way God was going to give him his call, so he was still seeking God about where to go. Then one night, he was standing in front of the trailer where he and Sandy were living on the Bible College campus, talking with Nola's father. Out of the clear, blue sky, it happened again. He said, "You and Sandy ought to go to Guatemala and be mission-aries." Jerry decided it was time to study some and at least find out exactly where this Guatemala was located. Maybe God was trying to tell him something.

One of the classes Jerry and Sandy took at the Bible College was Personal Evangelism. For that class, all the students went out two by two, knocked on doors and witnessed to people about the Lord. During this procedure, Sandy and her partner went to several homes and just "happened" to come upon a home of some returned missionaries. In San Antonio, a city of one million people, they just "happened" to come upon missionaries from Guatemala. Sandy and Jerry talked until the wee hours of the night and finally decided that God was calling them to Guatemala.

That was more than twenty-five years ago, and Jerry and Sandy have been working in Guatemala ever since. During all that time, they've never doubted that God "called" them to Guatemala. They were in Guatemala City when the earthquake hit that killed more than twenty-two thousand people. They've been in Guatemala when they could hear terrorists' bombs go off, bombs that would rattle the windows of their home. They've been in Guatemala when the guerrillas fired guns in their neighborhood. Their two daughters grew up in Guatemala, with the youngest one born there.

But during all this time, they've never doubted for a moment that God called them to Guatemala. God enabled them to open up three evangelistic centers in Guatemala, where evangelization is done on a daily basis. They use Christian literature, Bibles, music, films and a daily radio program to reach the people with the Gospel. They show an average of three films every day, 365 days of the year. Their film evangelism has covered every corner of the country of Guatemala and has moved up into the southern part of Mexico as well as extended down into the countries of Honduras and El Salvador.

A few years ago, the president of Guatemala, who was an evangelical Christian, took a man who was visiting his country to visit one of these evangelistic centers that Jerry and Sandy Owens had opened and operated. The visitor was none other than Carlos Salinas de Gortari, at that time the president of Mexico.

In 1986, Jerry felt the Lord would have them look beyond Central America into some of the other countries of South America, so he made a trip to visit Ecuador. One day sitting there on a park bench in downtown Quito, Ecuador, with the sun just going down behind the snow-capped mountains, Jerry felt the presence of the Lord remind him that of the thousands of people rushing past him on their way to their homes, only two of every hundred were believing Christians. He didn't have to pray long to see why God had spoken to his heart about going to Ecuador. So Jerry Owens began an outreach in Ecuador as well.

Seemingly things have come full circle. Jerry and Sandy's daughter, Karen, and her husband are now living and working in Guatemala, overseeing the work begun by her mother and father more than twenty-five years ago. Jerry Owens recently wrote the following tribute to Jerry Witt:

> "Jerry died at a very young age. Yet, it is not how many years you live, but how many lives you touch while you live. Jerry touched many lives and left his footprints in the sand of time. His hand print will not be on Hollywood Blvd., but you will find it on the souls of men. He touched my life to sell out all to Christ and be willing to go all the way with Him. He continues to touch my life as his son, Mark, and his team come to Ecuador to minister. Yes, 'Souls are crying, and men are dying.' There are other nations to conquer for Christ. Thousands have been saved because we answered the call ourselves. But, there are still millions still untold. Our conviction still is that we 'must win them to the Lord at any cost.' I trust that our eyes will always be wet with tears and that we will always have a heart of compassion until the world is evangelized."

Yes, one soldier fell in the battle, but dozens of others have been raised up to stand in his place. Another person who responded to the challenge of Jerry's death was his brother-in-law, Buddy Holder. Buddy was a student at International Bible College in San Antonio when Jerry was killed. One morning after I had spoken in the chapel service at the college, Buddy approached me with tears in his eyes and said he wanted to tell me about a dream he'd had a few nights earlier.

"It was like Jerry came to me and was telling me about the tremendous need for people to go and give the Gospel to those who have never heard," he said.

With his voice choked with tears, he continued, "And as we were standing there talking, Jerry reached out his hand to me and asked, 'Buddy, will you go?' "

As we stood there a few minutes in the emotion of the moment, Buddy regained control of his tears, and, as he lifted his head to look at me, I also looked at him and asked, "Well, Buddy. Will go you?"

Looking me square in the eye, he calmly answered, "Yes, I will."

And he did. Buddy spent eight years doing missionary work in the Torreon area. There are now two strong churches there as a result of Buddy's willingness to "go."

Again, one soldier fell, but numerous others were raised up to take his place.

One of the biggest surprises as we've continued our walk down the road of faith has been the way God has worked in the lives of our sons. Remember those three little boys: Jerry, age four; Mark, age two; and Philip, age seven months at the time of the airplane crash? They're all grown up now, young men with their own families, and they're all serving God.

Philip is married to a beautiful girl, Angela, from Canada. For several years, they lived in San Antonio, where he owned his own tile and marble business. Then they worked in a church in Toronto, Canada, for a couple of years, but a few years ago, they moved to the Atlanta, Georgia, area. They are on staff as youth pastors at a church in Dunwoody, Georgia. Their hope is to be able to minister also to the more than 500,000 Spanish-speaking people who live in the Atlanta area.

Jerry is a pilot and heads an organization he founded called HALUSA (Hasta Lo Ultimo De La Sierra, or *Unto the Uttermost Parts of the Mountains*), and it can truthfully be said that because of this work, thousands of Indians in the mountains of Mexico are receiving help and ministry that they never dreamed possible. Jerry works and ministers to numerous ethnic groups of the "forgotten people" of Mexico, the Indians who still live in spiritual darkness and bondage in the hard-to-reach mountains of Mexico.

One of these tribes, the Tepehuan Indians, lives in the state of Durango. They've been there for centuries, steeped in spiritual darkness. But the unusual thing about this group is that in all its centuries of history, there had never been even one single note of music written or sung in their language. None of their history or their legends. Not even a lullaby that the mothers used to sing their children to sleep. Nothing. This seems to have been unique with this group. The Gospel originally was taken into this tribe several years ago by some Wycliffe Translators, and although a few people had accepted Jesus, it was not the response that was desired and needed. Jerry began to work with these Wycliffe Translators and minister to the Tepehuan Indians. Then about five years ago, one of the Tepehuan Indians who was doing a prison term for cattle robbery received the Gospel at the hands of a missionary who witnessed to him while he was in prison. This man was converted and went back to the mountains with the story of salvation that was provided by the sacrifice of Jesus Christ. Little by little, as they heard more and began to respond to the ministry of this brother as well as to others such as our son, Jerry, things began to change with the Tepehuans. They began to sing in their own language. First, it was the Tepehuan brethren who knew both Spanish and Tepehuan who translated some of the choruses they had heard in Spanish and learned to sing them for the congregations. Then some of the more gifted ones began to play their guitars and write their own songs in their language. Now there is music, and only Christian music, being written and sung throughout the mountains where the Tepehuan brethren live.

About twenty people from the congregation in the city of Durango went with Jerry on one of these "brigades" up to the Tepehuan Indian tribe recently. It took almost fourteen hours to arrive at their destination, and although it was during May, by the time they had reached the high altitudes of the Sierra Madre Mountains, (ten-thousand-plus feet above sea level), it was cold. There was frost on the ground in the mornings. They slept in their thermals, sweats, jeans, sweaters, coats and a sleeping bag, and they were still cold.

On that particular brigade, they had four groups working in different areas of ministry. There was the Linguistic group, which was teaching the Tepehuans for the first time in history the Word of God in their own language.

There were those who worked with the children all day. With puppets, games and stories, the children were taught of the love of Jesus. The children had never seen balloons before, and they were fascinated by them. They spent hours just playing with an inflated balloon. Not being familiar with puppets, they were sometimes frightened, and those helping had to calm them down and explain to them what the puppet was.

There was an evangelistic group, which, during three or four gatherings each day, would use drama, movies and preaching to teach the adults the Word of God. Dozens of people accepted Jesus for the first time in their lives, and others received prayer and ministry for a particular problem they were facing.

There was the medical group, which ministered to the health care needs of those who came for help. All day, the doctors and helpers met with people and taught them how to boil water to avoid the dysentery that takes so many children's lives in the mountains. Lice was rampant, and many times, they would shave the children's heads to get rid of it, and the lice would be so thick that even though all the hair had been shaved, they would still cover the child's scalp. Scabies was everywhere. One two-year-old girl had scabies all over her body, even on her eyelids.

The ladies who had gone on the brigade were sleeping in an attic that had been put into the church building. They laid on the plain plank floors to sleep. The men slept in the vehicles. There were no bathroom facilities, only the trees and the mountains. Some of the men rigged up a thing where blankets were strung up around a big rock, and those who wanted a bath would stand on that rock behind the blankets and splash cold water over themselves.

Most of the Indians who came for the brigade's help had walked for hours to get there. They stayed the entire ten days that the group was in the mountains. They slept out in the open with their individual campfires.

At night, a person could look out across the mountains and through the forests and see dozens of little fires where these people were sleeping for the night. During the day, others came from nearby villages in trucks to receive help.

One of the young Tepehuan Christian men was named Modesto. He was interested in helping with the brigade in any way he could, but then he discovered the Linguistic group, and for the first time in his life, he learned to read and write in the Tepehuan language. He spent the rest of the brigade with the linguistic people and by the third day had mastered the mechanics of the language and was writing Bible stories in the Tepehuan language. That young man is now a pastor of a Tepehuan congregation.

This is an idea of what HALUSA is involved with all over Mexico. The groups have become much larger than the one to the Tepehuan Indians, and now the medical brigades include dentists, doctors, even surgeons. They still do the literacy work, teaching the Scriptures to the people in their own language, and evangelism is still the main emphasis of the effort. In 1995, HALUSA organized and administered some seven to eight brigades of two to six days each. They have ministered to the needs of the Purepecha Indians, the Amuzgo Indians, the Tarahumara and Guarijio, the Huichols, the Cora and, of course, the Tepehuan Indians. Just among the Purepecha and Amuzgo Indians alone, some three thousand to four thousand Indians have been ministered to with around two thousand conversions to the Lord Jesus Christ!

All this from the four-year-old boy who worried so about his younger brothers and who prayed for God to send him a daddy. Yes, Jerry Sr. fell in battle, but one of those raised up to take his place is his own son.

Another big surprise has been the way God is using Mark. Mark was the child in the middle, the two-year-old. All of our children studied music and became good musicians, but Mark decided to give his life to the composing, arranging, producing and distributing of Christian music for the Mexican church. It started out to be a ministry to the Mexican church but during the past few years has developed into a ministry for all of the Spanish-speaking churches in the world. In all the Spanish-speaking countries, beginning with Spain, to all of South America, through Central America, to Mexico and the Spanish-speaking population in the United States, it is not an exaggeration to say that Mark is the foremost musician and minister of praise and worship to the Spanish-speaking church, cutting across all denominational lines. His recordings have sold hundreds of thousands of copies, and his book, *Adoremos* (*Let Us Worship*), sold the most copies of all the Christian books in Spanish in 1994 and was named book of the year.

Recently, we were in Mexico City for one of Mark's Music Conferences, and although I had been told the number of people who were expected that night, nothing prepared me for the feeling of enormity that fifteen thousand people all gathered in one place brought. Even before we arrived in the auditorium where the meeting was to be held, we could hear a huge roar of voices all singing the praises of the Lord Jesus Christ. It took some time for our guide to lead us through the various tunnels, hallways, rooms, etc., but finally, we arrived to the spot reserved for us, immediately in front of the platform. The platform had been built super tall so all the people could see what was happening, so that we were looking up at the platform and the musicians and ministers who were located there. We had entered the auditorium at the second tier of seats, and it was from that vantage point, before we moved down onto the floor of the auditorium, that we were able to see and appreciate the enormity of this gathering. There was a huge sea of faces that began on the floor and continued up through five or six more layers to the roof of the auditorium. Their hands were lifted heavenward, and they were singing praises to Almighty God. It was overwhelming. And on the platform was the organizer and leader of this huge group of people, our son Mark Witt. In some places in South America, there have been as many as fifty thousand people who have attended these conferences. Recently, Mark helped organize and direct the music for the historical gathering "Homenaje a Jesus" ("Homage to Jesus") where some ninety-thousand people gathered in the Aztec Stadium in Mexico City to worship and praise God. Nothing like that had ever happened in the history of the country. Who would ever have thought that this was what God had planned for that two-year-old boy who used to cry whenever someone else cried.

One soldier fell, but dozens of others have been raised up to take his place.

And what can be said about the surprise that brought our beautiful twins, Jeannie and Lorie, into our lives and rounded our family off with their lovely feminine smiles and gentle ways? Jeannie and Lorie are adults now, also married and working in the ministry in Latin America. Both girls have done the vocal backgrounds on all of Mark's praise and worship recordings, and Lorie's husband, Coalo Zamorano, is the head of record production in Mexico for Latin America. Jeannie and her husband, Anthony (Naki) Theo, now head the leadership for the Bible school in Durango.

These are yet others who have been raised up to take the place of the fallen soldier.

Several years after Jerry was killed, Frank, Dub Williams and I were traveling down the highway that goes through the city of Sombrerete, where Jerry's and Nicolas' bodies were held that terrible day in April 1964. Dub had been part of the group who had gone down to Sombrerete to pick up their bodies, and although he didn't speak enough Spanish in those days to understand everything that was happening, it didn't take much Spanish to understand the animosity and hostility that was demonstrated toward the men who made that trip. The highway we were traveling skirted the edge of the town and passed in front of the city cemetery where the bodies had been held. I had never known exactly where their bodies had been held, so Frank and I asked Dub to point out the location to us. He did, and as he began to answer Frank's questions about some of the things that had happened that day, it was like I was carried back in my mind and in my emotions to that terrible time, and for a few minutes, I again felt in my heart the pain and the weight of that loss. It was only for a few minutes, almost as though God was reminding me of just how far He had brought me since that devastating news was brought to my front door.

In Hebrews 12, there is mention of a "cloud of witnesses" that surrounds us. I like to think that Jerry is a part of that "cloud of witnesses" and that as he looks down from heaven at what has happened in this part of the world he loved so much, and at what has happened in my life through my marriage to Frank and the birth of the twins, and at what is going on now in the lives of his sons, he smiles and is happy with what he sees.

Jerry was one soldier who fell in battle. But God has used that fall to raise up others to take his place. The battle goes on, and the Church continues to march forward.

Jerry Witt, in1958; a young man whose primary passion was to serve the Lord.

Jerry Witt standing in front of the plane in which he would later have an accident. The two children are the children of a local Mexican pastor with whom Jerry worked.

Jerry's y Nola's wedding day on July 1959. From left to right: Lottie Holder, Nola's grandmother; Eugene Holder, Nola's father; Loren Holder, Nola's mother; Nola; Jerry; W. L. Cole; Nola's grandfather; Nola M. Cole; Nola's grandmother.

Nola and Jerry singing together two weeks before the fatal accident.

Nola and Jerry in a family picture taken in December 1963. The children left to right are: Felipe, Marcos and Jerry Jr. This would be the last picture taken as a family.

In the fall of 1966 the children pose for a picture. Left to right: Jerry Jr., Felipe, and Marcos.

The boys enjoy a day at an amusement park in Guadalajara, Mexico. From left to right: Felipe, Marcos and Jerry Jr.

Frank Warren's arrival brought much stability to Nola's life and the boy's lives. From left to right: Marcos, Nola, Felipe, Frank and Jerry Jr.

In time came God's other gift: the twins. Here is Jeanie (background) and Lorena (foreground) on the piano; they, like their brothers, learned to play music on this piano. Their teacher was Nola.

In 1978, the "Witt Trio" shows their favorite instruments. From left to right: Jerry Jr., Felipe and Marcos.

Jerry Jr. and Vicky Witt with their two children: Michelle and Jerry Witt, III. Jerry is a pilot and ministry director of HALUSA (acrostic in Spanish for "Unto the Uttermost Parts of the Mountains.").

Marcos and Miriam Witt their four children (left to right): Kristofer, Jonathan, Miriam, Marcos, Carlos and Elena. Marcos is a renowned international minster and worship leader.

Jeannie (Warren)
and Anthony (Naki)
Theo.

John Anthony Theo,
Naki's and Jeannie's son.

Lorena (Warren)
and Coalo
Zamorano with
their daughter,
Laurene.

Felipe and Angela Witt with their two oldest children: Drew and Charity. Missing is the new baby girl, Destiny.

Today, Frank and Nola Warren can testify of God's faithfulness and love with them and their family.

Notes

CHAPTER 1:
IN THE BEGINNING

1. Archie recently passed away at the ripe old age of sixty-two. He was one of the longest living hemophiliacs on record.

2. Each student was required to donate 30 minutes of work time each day doing something around the campus. My job was helping to serve breakfast.

CHAPTER 2:
"HERE WE ARE, YOU LUCKY PEOPLE"

3. For a fuller explanation of this type of flying, please see chapter three.

4. A carry-all was a combination of a station wagon and a pick-up truck. It would compare with today's Jeep Wagoneer or Suburban. The carry-all we had was old and worn out.

CHAPTER 3:

THE END OF THE BEGINNING

5. W. W. Williams, personal letter, Durango, Durango, Mexico, February 15, 1994.

6. Jerry D. Witt, Jr., personal interview with mayor of town, Las Minas Coloradas, Zacatecas, February, 1994.

7. Spanish for "invaders."

8. Daniel Gutierrez, personal letter and interview, Tijuana, Baja California Norte, June 30, 1994.

9. Dan Petker, personal letter from Yerington, Nevada, January, 1994.

10. Daniel Gutierrez, personal letter and interview, Tijuana, Baja California Norte, June 30, 1994.

11. W. W. Williams, personal letter, From Leesville, Louisiana, February, 1994.

CHAPTER 5:
PICKING UP THE PIECES

12. "machismo"—The man is always the boss, regardless of the circumstances. For example, if a mother is left a widow, there are times when even her child, if he is a male, is the one who will make the decisions.

13.	A loss of time. An embarrassing or awkward situation.
14.	Unlimited, unconditional, all out surrender
	This is my Father's plan for me
	I love Him, and I give Him all that He asks
	"In dedication, Lord, to Thee."

CHAPTER 6:
"¡Asi es la Vida!"

15.	That's life!
16.	What makes this interesting is that after Frank and I were married, we left for our honeymoon on the coast of Mexico and had three flat tires before we arrived back home in Durango!
17.	Name has been changed.
18.	Name has been changed.
19.	Twenty-six years later while I was doing a concert with Mark in a large city in Mexico, a lady came running up to me at the end of the performance, threw her arms around me and began to weep. I had no idea who she was, but I just held her and let her get control of herself. Finally, standing back and looking at me, she asked, "Do you know who I am?" Looking at her closely, I said, "No, I'm afraid I don't recognize you." Holding my upper arms, she shook me a little and said, "Look more closely." Taking an even closer look at her, I told her that she looked familiar but that I still didn't know who she was. Smiling a little, she said, "I am Ana." My mouth fell open as I asked, "Robert's mother?" "Yes," she said. It turned out that she and her husband had been separated for several years and that he and Robert were together living a life of sin, but that she and her daughters were together and they were serving God and attending church regularly in the city where they lived. "You know," I told her, "there were some problems between us the last time we saw each other." Clasping me to her and bursting into tears again, she said, "I know, I know. But, forgive us, and let us put all that in the past."

CHAPTER 7:
VICTORY AND DEFEAT

20.	A "machete" is a heavy, curved knife about two to three feet in length, that is used for everything from cutting wood to butchering a pig.
21.	This was necessary since we worked with poor people who had no vehicles nor any idea of how to drive a car or truck.
22.	The three bedrooms all opened onto the same small hallway which also led to the winding stairway that went downstairs. Karen, the boys and I had all been sleeping in our respective bedrooms before this episode took place.